Community

Welfare, Crime and Society

This book is part of a series published by Open University Press in association with The Open University. The three books in the *Welfare, Crime and Society* series are:

Social Justice: Welfare, Crime and Society (edited by Janet Newman and Nicola Yeates)

Security: Welfare, Crime and Society (edited by Allan Cochrane and Deborah Talbot)

Community: Welfare, Crime and Society (edited by Gerry Mooney and Sarah Neal)

This publication forms part of the Open University course *Welfare, crime and society* (DD208). Details of this and other Open University courses can be obtained from the Student Registration and Enquiry Service, The Open University, PO Box 197, Milton Keynes, MK7 6BJ, United Kingdom; tel. +44 (0)845 300 6090; email general-enquiries@open.ac.uk

Alternatively, you may visit the Open University website at http://www.open.ac.uk where you can learn more about the wide range of courses and packs offered at all levels by The Open University.

To purchase a selection of Open University course materials visit http://www.ouw.co.uk, or contact Open University Worldwide Ltd, Walton Hall, Milton Keynes MK7 6AA, United Kingdom for a brochure, tel. +44 (0)1908 858785; fax +44 (0)1908 858787; email ouw-customer-services@open.ac.uk

Community

Welfare, Crime and Society

Edited by Gerry Mooney and Sarah Neal

Open University Press in association with The Open University

Open University Press
McGraw-Hill Education
McGraw-Hill House
Shoppenhangers Road
Maidenhead
Berkshire
England
SL6 2QL

Email: enquiries@openup.co.uk
world wide web: www.openup.co.uk

and Two Penn Plaza, New York, NY 10121–2289, USA

First published 2009

A catalogue record of this book is available from the British Library.

ISBN 0 3352 2934 4 *paperback*

ISBN 978 0 3352 2934 5 *paperback*

ISBN 0 3352 2933 6 *hardback*

ISBN 978 0 3352 2933 8 *hardback*

Library of Congress Cataloguing-in-Publication Data

CIP data applied for.

Edited and designed by The Open University.

Typeset in India by Alden Prepress Services, Chennai.

Printed and bound in the United Kingdom by Bell & Bain Ltd., Glasgow.

1.1

Contents

Notes on contributors

John Clarke is Professor of Social Policy at The Open University. His recent books include *Changing Welfare, Changing States* (Sage, 2004) and *Creating Citizen-Consumers: Changing Publics and Changing Public Services* (with Janet Newman; Sage, 2007). He is currently writing *Publics, Politics and Power: Remaking the Public in Public Services* (with Janet Newman; Sage, 2009).

Allan Cochrane is Professor of Urban Studies at The Open University. He is author of *Understanding Urban Policy* (Blackwell, 2007) and (with John Allen and Doreen Massey) of *Rethinking the Region* (Routledge, 1998), as well as editor (with John Clarke and Sharon Gewirtz) of *Comparing Welfare States* (Sage, 2001).

Gordon Hughes is Professor of Criminology at the Cardiff School of Social Sciences, Cardiff University, Wales. His recent books include *The Politics of Crime and Community* (Palgrave Macmillan, 2007), *Restorative Justice* (co-edited; Sage, 2003), *Criminological Perspectives* (co-edited; Sage, 2003). He is currently writing a monograph: *Sociology and Crime: Towards a New Criminological Imagination* (Sage). He is co-editor of *Criminology and Criminal Justice: An International Journal* (Sage) and is a member of the editorial board of the *British Journal of Criminology* (Oxford).

Gerry Mooney is Senior Lecturer in Social Policy and Staff Tutor, Social Sciences, at The Open University in Scotland. He is author (with Iain Ferguson and Michael Lavalette) of *Rethinking Welfare* (Sage, 2002) and editor (with Gill Scott) of *Exploring Social Policy in the 'New' Scotland* (The Policy Press, 2005) and (with Alex Law) of *New Labour/Hard Labour?* (The Policy Press, 2007).

Sarah Neal is Senior Lecturer in Social Policy at The Open University. Her books include *The Making of Equal Opportunities Policies in Universities* (Open University Press, 1998), *The New Countryside: Ethnicity, Nation and Exclusion in Contemporary Rural Britain* (edited with Julian Agyeman; The Policy Press, 2006), *Rural Identities: Ethnicity and Community in the Contemporary English Countryside* (Ashgate, 2008) and *Race, Multiculture and Social Policy* (Palgrave Macmillan, 2010).

Janet Newman is Professor of Social Policy at The Open University. Her publications include *The Managerial State* (with John Clarke; Sage, 1997); *Modernising Governance: New Labour, Policy and Society* (Sage, 2001); *Remaking Governance: Peoples, Politics and the Public Sphere* (The Policy Press, 2005); *Power, Participation and Political Renewal* (with Marian Barnes and Helen Sullivan; The Policy Press, 2007) and *Creating Citizen-Consumers: Changing Publics and Changing Public Services* (with John Clarke et al.; Sage, 2007).

Sharon Pinkney is Senior Lecturer in Social Policy and Staff Tutor, Social Sciences, at The Open University in Yorkshire. She has twelve years' teaching experience at The Open University and previous experience in social and welfare work. Her current research is on constructions of children's and young people's participation in social care contexts. She has previously published in the fields of reconstructing social care, children and young people and participation rights.

Esther Saraga is Senior Lecturer and Staff Tutor, Social Sciences, at The Open University with thirty-six years' experience of teaching mature students in higher education. She is currently engaged in an (auto) biographical research project around her parents' flight from Nazi Germany. Previous research and publications have included constructions of childhood in relation to social policy, and feminist approaches to child sexual abuse.

Nicola Yeates is Senior Lecturer in Social Policy at The Open University. Her recent books include *Globalisation and Social Policy* (Sage, 2001), *Understanding Global Social Policy* (The Policy Press, 2008) and *Migrant Workers and Globalising Care Economies: Explorations in Global Care Chains* (Palgrave Macmillan, 2009). She is co-editor of *Global Social Policy: an interdisciplinary journal of public policy and social development* (Sage) and a member of the international advisory board of *Translocations: The Irish migration, race and social transformation review* (www.imrstr.dcu.ie).

Series preface

Community: Welfare, Crime and Society is the third of three books in a new series of textbooks published by Open University Press in association with The Open University. The series, entitled *Welfare, Crime and Society*, is designed to provide a social scientific understanding of the complex and fascinating entanglements between the worlds of social welfare and crime control. At the heart of the series is the suggestion that it is difficult to draw a clear line between social welfare and crime control. These entanglements are examined in respect of ideas, institutions, policies and practices – and their effects and impacts. The series extends beyond national borders to look at other societies and the policy concerns and developments that link them to present-day United Kingdom. The series uses different sources of evidence to understand these trends and their effects, and it examines how evidence is mobilised in the course of research, evaluation and policymaking.

The three books in this series are as follows:

- *Social Justice: Welfare, Crime and Society*, edited by Janet Newman and Nicola Yeates. This book explores ways of defining and enacting social justice in the context of social welfare and crime control strategies. It examines how the notion of social justice informs experiences and understandings of the social world, why it appeals to so many people as a mobilising ideal for social change and policy reform, and how it shapes claims, demands and actions people take in the pursuit of the 'good society'.

- *Security: Welfare, Crime and Society*, edited by Allan Cochrane and Deborah Talbot. This book focuses on the ways in which security as an idea, an ideal and a practice can shed light on the entanglements and intersections between welfare and crime, and the ambiguities, tensions and contradictions that arise from them. The book is concerned specifically with the increasingly blurred area between social welfare and crime control policies and the ways in which it is managed.

- *Community: Welfare, Crime and Society*, edited by Gerry Mooney and Sarah Neal. At the heart of this book is an examination of the unique ability of the idea of community to work effectively as shorthand for collective well-being and positive social relations, and as a means of categorising social problems and 'problem populations'. It is this paradox that makes the idea of community a valuable lens for understanding the diverse and complex ways in which social welfare policies and crime control policies collide.

Each book is self-contained and can be read on its own or studied as part of a wide range of courses in universities and colleges. Because these books are integral elements of an Open University course (*Welfare, crime and society*), they are designed as interactive teaching texts to meet the needs of distance learners. The chapters form a planned sequence: each chapter builds on its predecessors. References backwards and forwards to other books and book chapters in the series are highlighted in bold type. Each chapter concludes with a set of suggestions for further reading in relation to its core topics. The chapters are also organised around a number of student-friendly exercises that encourage active learning:

■ *Activities*: highlighted in colour, these are exercises which invite the reader to take an active part in working on the text and are intended to develop understanding and reflective analysis;

■ *Comments*: these provide feedback from the chapter's author(s) on the activities and enable the reader to compare their responses with the thoughts of the author(s).

The production of this book, and the two others that make up the series, draws on the expertise of a wide range of people beyond its editors and authors. Each book reflects the combined efforts of an Open University course team: the 'collective teacher' at the heart of the Open University's educational system. The Open University academics on the *Welfare, crime and society* course team are mainly based in the Department of Social Policy and Criminology in the Faculty of Social Sciences. Each chapter in these books has been through a thorough process of drafting and review to refine both its contents and its teaching approach. This process of development leaves us indebted to the consultant authors, tutor advisors and the course assessor. It also brings together and benefits from a range of other skills and expertise – secretarial staff, editors, designers, audio and video producers, librarians – to translate the ideas into the finished product. All of these activities are held together by the course team manager and course team chairs who ensure that all these component parts fit together successfully. Our thanks to all the contributors to this series.

Sarah Neal and Nicola Yeates, Series Editors

Chapter 1
Community: themes and debates

Gerry Mooney and Sarah Neal

Contents

1   Introduction

We begin this book with a very obvious question: why does it make sense to examine the concept, or idea, of community in order to understand the contemporary relationship between welfare strategies and crime control strategies? Although this may seem a straightforward question, it is rather telling that we need a whole book to answer it adequately.

'Community' is a familiar term that is used in a variety of everyday contexts and conversations. It is often used to refer to 'good' social relations because it suggests connected groups of people who care about and for each other. It is this idea of care and social bonds that puts community firmly in the realm of what we might mean by the terms 'welfare' and 'social well-being'. As anthropologists Vered Amit and Nigel Rapport (2002, p. 13) note, the term 'community' has far more '*emotional resonance* than a more utilitarian term like "group"'. The social theorist Zigmunt Bauman (2001, p. 1) makes a similar point when he describes the idea of community as being 'like a fireplace at which we warm our hands on a frosty day'. The association between the concept of community and collective care, security and well-being is the first reason why this book is about community.

However, community can also be mobilised, or purposely used, to categorise groups of people in a negative way; that is, it can have less positive connotations. There are several different ways in which it is possible to see this working. First, community can be used to describe groups of people who are perceived to be too bounded, too closed off or separate from wider society. In other words, they have *too much* community. This can be a cause for concern in terms of social integration, social cohesion and social order. Second, communities that have a strong sense of identity can be hostile towards and suspicious of those who are seen as 'outsiders'. In this way community can be exclusionary. Third, because community is about the group rather than the individual, communities can constrain individual freedom and be intolerant of difference. And fourth, community is also the term often used to describe people in relation to social conflict, deprivation and disadvantaged places.

The association between the concept of community and social problems is the second reason why this book is about community. 'Community' can work as 'shorthand' for collective social welfare and social order, and, equally, for collective social troubles and social *dis*order. Because of this, the concept of community has been of much interest in social and crime policy thinking and interventions. It is in this context that the aims of this book are to:

■   examine the *different meanings* attached to the concept of community and the debates as to its definitions

- explore why the concept of community has such *positive associations* and *widespread appeal*

- understand how community can be used to identify 'problem populations' *and* as the basis for responding to such populations

- look at some of the ways in which community has played a *significant role* in social welfare policy and crime control policy

- discuss how the concept of community has been researched in the social sciences, and consider how policymakers have *engaged with evidence* about communities.

Drawing on a mixture of case study examples and using social science research, policy texts and memoir to illustrate its arguments, this first chapter focuses on the competing ways in which community can be interpreted, and discusses some of the theoretical approaches to understanding what community means. Aspects of these theoretical approaches will inform and reappear in the rest of the chapters in the book.

The structure of this chapter reflects these tasks. Section 2 discusses the contested status of the concept of community. Section 3 outlines four theoretical ways for thinking about community. Developing these discussions, Section 4 looks at the idea of social capital, and suggests that social capital has emerged from the community 'stable' and has an increasingly integrated presence in policy and political discourses of community. The emphasis on the relationship between evidence, the concept of community and policymaking is a thread that runs through both Chapter 1 and all the remaining chapters in the book, which are outlined briefly in Section 5.

2   The different meanings of community

We began this chapter by asking a seemingly straightforward question and have already begun to hint at some of the challenges that are raised by any attempt to set out what community might mean to laypeople, scholars, policymakers and governments. Finding one definitive meaning of community is neither possible nor desirable. What we will suggest is that a robust social science response to this question will vary (community may mean very different things to different people); it will be context specific (community will 'look' different and can change according to particular settings and particular environments); and it will be conditional (community will be shaped by economic, political and historical moments). So any response to the question 'what is community?' will stress that it is not possible to reduce community to a single set of generally applicable criteria. Sarah Neal and Sue Walters

(2008, p. 280) have argued that given its multiple meanings, 'community needs to come with a sociological health warning' in order to flag the different ways in which it is used and understood.

Activity 1.1

Take a few minutes and think through some different types of groups that are described, or describe themselves, as a community. Make a brief note on one or two of those groups you thought of, and reflect on why you would describe them as a community.

Comment

You may have come up with definitions that use *place* as the basis of community – the neighbourhood, your street, your town or village, or your part of a city. Cities themselves can be described as communities. This is particularly so at times of crisis. New York at the time of the destruction of the Twin Towers on 11 September 2001, for instance, was regularly spoken of in terms of a community under attack. London was described in similar terms after the bombings on 7 July 2005, and during the Blitz in the Second World War. You may also have defined a group as a community because of its *identity* – a minority or majority ethnic community (e.g. English, Bangladeshi, Polish or Caribbean); the lesbian and gay community; a religious or faith community (e.g. Jewish or Catholic). You may have described community through *institutions* where you work or attend – the university community, the artistic or business community. Or, you may have thought of community through *politics* – the national community – nations can be and are presented as communities that have a shared history, language and set of values. This can be extended to what is referred to as the 'international community' – a collection of like-minded nations seemingly agreeing or working together over a particular issue. This frequently has an institutional frame – the United Nations or the Commonwealth, for instance. You might have understood community through *technology*. The notion of online or cyber communities, in which people are able to interact without any spatial or face-to-face contact, but through virtual communication, is of increasing interest in the study of community.

There are, of course, many other examples, but it is the extent to which the term 'community' can be stretched and pulled in order to describe very different sets of social relations that is important. Community can be a local area and the familiarity of face-to-face contact; it can refer to the ways in which individuals connect with others (whom they may not know or ever meet); and it can be a political tool and way of organising that expresses a mutual approach between and across sovereign nations.

Figure 1.1

Images of community: talking over a garden fence, 1951; Notting Hill Carnival, London, 2006; a Golden Jubilee street party, London, 2002

Although it is used in such very diverse ways, what brings together all these conceptions of community is the notion of something shared or held in common. This idea of social bonds is a key marker for the concept of community. It is perhaps this more than anything else that forms the basis of why the concept of community has such widespread and different appeal. Community seems to connote a social commonality or togetherness. As we have discussed, this can be read in very different ways. It can be problematic and highly exclusionary ('us' and 'them'), although community tends, in everyday, in policy and in political discourse, to be positively cast and mobilised. A good example of this is captured in one of the recommendations of the Report of the Commission on Integration and Cohesion, published in 2007. The Commission was set up by the UK government to address the ways in which local and national social cohesion in a multicultural society could be achieved effectively (see Chapter 2). The Report urges the development of a nationally sponsored 'Community Week':

> A nationally sponsored 'Community Week' with a focus on celebrating all communities and inter-community engagement should start early in 2008 ... This week could be a time for individual faith and other groups to open their doors to each other – moving from a focus on school twinning towards twinning of places of worship, places of employment and twinning of existing neighbourhood groups and projects. It could be an opportunity to run inexpensive neighbours' events such as street parties, garden fetes or jumble sales. Every locality will do this differently and rightly so.
> (Commission on Integration and Cohesion, 2007, section 8, para. 10, p. 114)

We can see how the idea of community is being used here as a way through which the locally based interaction and integration of people can be established and developed. The emphasis is on shared spaces (twinning), open institutions (places of worship, work) and fun (street parties, fetes). In making this policy recommendation, the intention is to encourage social connectedness both between the local areas in which people live and between individuals, their neighbours and other residents. In this policy vision, community delivers not only socially connected communities, but also social stability.

A similarly positive conception of community is also part of everyday discourse. To illustrate this, we have included a short extract from a focus group interview conducted for a research project in which one of us (Sarah Neal) was involved. The project was an investigation of identity and social change in rural England. The participants in the focus group interviews were all members of the local Young Farmers' Clubs and Women's Institutes.

Extract 1.1

Lee: *I've lived on a farm in White Ford all my life. I've never wanted to live*
in Highton [the nearest large town in the area]. I found that there's like
a better community spirit around here. The people you've grown up with
and went to school with and stuff and you know their parents and their
families and everything and there's always stuff to do everyday. People
get together and you know them all as well.

Researcher: *And that's important?*

Lee: *Yeah.*

Neal and Walters, 2007, p. 254

What is apparent straight away is the way in which the idea of
community is used by Lee to describe experiences of face-to-face contact,
mutual support and interdependency. These descriptions chime directly
with the aims of the national community week recommendations of the
Commission on Integration and Cohesion. Amit and Rapport (2002,
pp. 58–9) argue that most of us acquire our sense of community and
belonging through the mundane routines of everyday life, 'our
neighbours, the parents at our children's school, or team mates, fellow
students, club members, conference-goers and more'.

However, reading the interview extract again, what also comes out
strongly is Lee's description of the *feeling*, or having a *sense*, of
community. This is important to note. Community can work not only
as *enacted* social relations (e.g. having a chat over the garden fence,
organising a street party, or helping out when a neighbour is ill). It is
also present as a *potential* set of social interactions (e.g. when people
refer to a *sense* of community, of there being a 'community spirit'). In
this way, we could say that, in the interview extract above, community
was an *imagined* as much as a *material* presence. In other words, the
social bonds do not necessarily have to be continually enacted; if not
more important is people's *perception* that they exist (see also
Chapter 5).

The idea that the connections between people can be imagined means
that community can move away from a particular place and the social
practices that occur there. Community is then used as a way to describe
the social relations we think we have with others who share the same
ethnicity, cultural practices and religious or political affiliation, for
example. Developing or establishing connections with others, and
a sense of belonging through geography and/or through identity,

involves defining oneself against something else – in other words, defining *what I am not* as well as *what I am*. In this way, community, as you will see below, is always, at some level, inevitably about boundaries and outsiders. Of course, such boundaries and related exclusionary practices can shift and change, but the idea of processes in which some people are included while others are excluded is crucial to understanding what community means and why it is relevant to making sense of the connections between social welfare provision and crime control strategies.

Extract 1.2 is an example of what community boundaries look like in everyday life. This extract, from an interview with Harry Bernstein, a Russian Jew now living in the USA, appeared in *The Guardian* newspaper in 2007. Bernstein has written an autobiographical memoir of growing up in Stockport, England before and during the First World War (Bernstein, 2007). Bernstein's family were refugees from the pogroms in Eastern Europe and the memoir is an account of his childhood and what it was like to be a Jewish refugee living in Stockport's East Street.

Extract 1.2

Harry Bernstein knows all about walls. You might say he was a connoisseur of forced separation, of the erection of barriers to keep people apart. But the walls he knows so well are not physical ... Bernstein is an expert on the walls of the mind. He spent his childhood at the time of the first world war living in the shadow of just such a wall. It ran down the middle of his street in the Lancashire mill town of Stockport, between two rows of tenements and though there were no markers to line its route, it might have been 10 feet high for the number of times people crossed it.

The wall that ran down East Street was religion: Jews lived in one row of houses, Christians in the other ...

...

Bernstein can only speak for one side of the street because his contact with the other was so limited. He says that the prevailing feeling within his family was that the Christians were somehow beneath them. While they worked in the mills, the Jewish men were tailors; while the Christians wore iron-shod clogs, the Jews aspired to leather shoes.

The cruel irony of such judgments was that, in truth, both sides were locked into unspeakable poverty ...

'You would think that poverty was a leveller that would drag all of us down to the same depth. But it wasn't like that,' Bernstein says.

There were points at which the rigid culture of the divide softened and a passage through the wall was permitted, albeit within strict limits. On Friday and Saturday nights the Jewish families would have to call on their Christian neighbours across the way to light their fires for them – in return for some small change – as they were forbidden to do so themselves on the Sabbath.

Pilkington, 2007, pp. 12–13

Bernstein's account is important to us here because it shows how divisions within communities are able to work at a very micro level – his story concerns one street. This is significant because we have argued that streets are often the sites in which we feel or experience community (see also Chapters 3 and 5). Bernstein's account shows not only the boundary between two communities, but also that this boundary is unaffected by the shared experience of extreme poverty in East Street. We will return to the question of community as a boundary in the next section.

Figure 1.2
Harry Bernstein with the Swedish edition of his autobiography *The Invisible Wall*; a street in Stockport in the early 1900s

3 Theoretical approaches to community

As well as being one of the most contested, community is also one of the oldest social science concepts. However, the challenges of defining community, and of being able to identify communities empirically in the social world, have meant that by the 1970s, some social theorists declared that community as a concept should be jettisoned, because it was neither theoretically nor empirically useful. Social changes, such as increased mobility, migration, individualism and a growing visibility of the different experiences of people within communities, all meant that community became a category from which scholars distanced themselves. For example, the sociologist Margaret Stacey argued in 1969 that community studies were largely descriptive and that the concept of community was not capable of accounting for the complexities of social organisation and practices (Stacey, 1969). The geographer Doreen Massey (1994) has also pointed out that even within the seemingly stable homogeneity of a small mining community, the experiences of community will be very differently shaped by a range of other factors – for example, the spaces in which women move and meet will be different from those in which men move and meet. Problematising the concept of community in this way raises questions as to whether it has reliable explanatory value in understanding social relations.

Despite these doubts, the announcements of the death of community do appear as somewhat premature. In academic study, community continues to be much written about and researched; in everyday contexts, community is a term and idea that is widely used; and in politics and policymaking, community has become increasingly central to the ways in which populations are managed and policies delivered. This section will discuss four key and connected approaches to community: community as spatially based; community as identity-based; community as boundary; and community as a site of governance and policy intervention.

3.1 Community as a spatial concept: locality and belonging

In Extract 1.1 in the previous section, we used interview data to describe how it felt to be part of a community. What Lee also spoke of in that extract was his feeling of attachment to White Ford as a particular place. Extract 1.3 is from another interview from that same research project, and provides an even clearer example of attachment to a geographical place.

Extract 1.3

Elsa: *All my children ... were brought up here and I'm so interested that they have all come back to live near because it is such a happy village ...*

Sheila: *When we bought our house the three previous owners of it all still lived in Little Greening ... so people, once they get here don't want to move away.*

> *Researcher:* So what is it about Little Greening then? You've mentioned that it is a happy village, you've mentioned that. Tell me again about why.
>
> *Elsa:* I think that it is very supportive. [Murmurs of agreement]. Yes, we all support each other and know what's going on.

Neal and Walters, 2006, p. 186

Figure 1.3
Rural villages are closely linked with the concept of community: Much Hadham, Hertfordshire

We selected this extract because the conversation clearly shows the ways in which it is living in Little Greening that forms the basis of the participants' feelings of social well-being and belonging. The attachments that people feel to the places in which they live are a mix of the geographical ('A happy village') and the social (family, friends, resources, amenities). In particular, ideas of family and kinship are often closely associated with notions of community (**McCarthy, 2008**; see also Chapter 3 in this volume).

Activity 1.2

Table 1.1 is taken from research conducted by a team of sociologists studying sense of belonging in four different areas surrounding the city of Manchester (Savage et al., 2005). It shows the relationship between having a sense of belonging and where residents had come from – whether they were 'local', or had come from Manchester itself, the surrounding region or from further away. The figures are the percentage of the number of participating residents in the five categories. The number of people for each category is shown in parentheses. Consider what the figures in the table tell us about feelings of belonging.

Table 1.1 Percentage of participants brought up in different places who feel they belong in the area of current residence

	Cheadle	Chorlton	Ramsbottom	Wilmslow
Brought up locally	45 (22)	50 (6)	81 (11)	36 (8)
Brought up in Manchester area	64 (11)	67 (9)	63 (8)	50 (5)
Brought up in the north/mids*	43 (7)	63 (16)	50 (20)	79 (19)
Brought up elsewhere in England	0 (2)	56 (9)	33 (3)	20 (5)
Brought up outside England	0 (0)	43 (7)	67 (3)	50 (6)
Total 'belonging'	48 (42)	58 (47)	60 (45)	60 (43)
Total who are emphatic in stating that they do not belong	10 (42)	11 (47)	11 (45)	9 (43)

[* Midlands.]

Source: Savage et al., 2005, p. 47, Table 2.5

Comment

The most important finding that you may have observed is the high percentage (as shown in the Total 'belonging' category), across all four areas, of research participants who felt that they belonged to their area of residence. Perhaps most striking is the Wilmslow sample, where the majority of participants (19) had moved into Wilmslow from elsewhere in the north of England or the Midlands, but in this category 79 per cent expressed a high score on their sense of belonging. Ramsbottom is also interesting. Of those residents who had been brought up locally (11), 81 per cent had an established sense of belonging to the area. What the table also shows is that having a sense of belonging to a place is not necessarily about being 'local', although it may be so. The table can be understood to reflect, in a very different way, some of the sentiments that were expressed in the earlier interview extract about the importance of place and belonging.

The approach to understanding community as place based, or as a *spatial* concept, dominated theories of community up until the 1970s. Community was what 'happened' when a group of people lived together in the same place. Locally based social practices and bonds depended on face-to-face interaction between people who knew each other, or who were familiar and recognised by each other, were sometimes related to each other and, to a certain extent, were dependent on each other.

One of the earliest and best known theories of community was that developed by the nineteenth-century German sociologist Ferdinand Tönnies. In analysing the impact that industrialisation was making on European societies, Tönnies (1963) saw that social relations were being transformed as largely rural-based populations began to move to expanding cities in response to economic change. He identified two distinct sets of social relations – *Gemeinschaft*, the term he used to describe rurally and locally based unified and traditional community; and *Gesellschaft*, the term he used to describe urbanised, fragmented and modern society. Tönnies understood community as human togetherness formed through the convergence of: the biological (family), the geographical (rural place), the sociological (everyday interaction and dependency) and the psychological (attachment and a sense of belonging) (Bell and Newby, 1971). The concepts of *Gemeinschaft* and *Gesellschaft* were in oppositional conflict as *Gemeinschaft* social relations became increasingly redundant and rare in the face of industrial capitalism.

Although Tönnies may have overemphasised the unity of rural communities and failed to anticipate the forms of *Gemeinschaft* social relations that would become established in urban environments, his definition of community has been influential and has achieved status as a classic theory. For early urban sociologists, towns and cities have offered places or neighbourhoods in which – despite the heterogeneity and size of the city – community-based social relations could be identified. These urban neighbourhoods were overlaid by other identity factors, such as ethnicity, religion or occupation. This emphasis on localities within urban environments as the basis of community can be seen in the work of North American, University of Chicago-based sociologists, such as Robert Park, Earnest Burgess and Louis Wirth, in the 1920s and 1930s. This approach to sociology, which became known as the Chicago School, argued that in spite of the extent of difference and the seeming individualism of urban environments, community had not disappeared from the social relations of the city. For example, for Park (1915, p. 608) the city offered 'a mosaic of little worlds which touch but do not interpenetrate'. Further, community research associated with scholars such as Michael Young and Peter Willmott, who worked on family and kinship in Bethnal Green in London during the slum clearances of the 1950s, also argued that a *Gemeinschaft* community based on locality, family and everyday interaction was very much in evidence in the terraced streets of London's East End (Young and Willmott, 1957). (You will find more about studies of community in Chapter 3.)

Activity 1.3

Take a moment to think of examples of areas in cities that might be associated with particular communities. This is *not* to say that all the people who live in those places are of the same community, of course (see Figure 1.4). Rather, the aim of this activity is to emphasise that it is possible for communities to be spatially located within urban settings (again, see Figure 1.4).

Comment

You may have selected a particular area on the basis of class, religion, historical associations or ethnicity, or different mixes of all or some of these. If we consider London, for example, we might think of the East End and link that area with poor white English communities, formerly with Jewish refugee communities and contemporarily with Bangladeshi communities (this is discussed further Chapter 3). Similarly, areas within other cities across the UK – for instance, the Gorbals in Glasgow or Lochee in Dundee – have historically been linked with Irish migration.

Doreen Massey (cited in Cresswell, 2004, pp. 63–70) has written in similar terms about Kilburn, a small area of north-west London. Although Kilburn is closely associated with Irish migration, Massey describes walking down Kilburn High Road and seeing evidence of the presence of other communities – the shop selling saris, and posters advertising a bhangra night next to posters advertising Irish bands, for example. Massey explains that while Kilburn does have 'a character of its own', it 'absolutely does not have a seamless coherent identity, a single sense of place' (quoted in Cresswell, 2004, p. 68). The various populations and people who live in Kilburn live in it differently – they may use different shops and amenities, and have different affections and connections within and to Kilburn. As Massey suggests, this difference can be 'a source of richness and a source of conflict' (quoted in Cresswell, 2004, p. 68), but it also emphasises that places and communities are mixed together in complex ways, and the points of sameness and identity are not necessarily spatially fixed.

Although we are suggesting that community cannot be understood only in terms of space and place, we are emphasising here that approaches to community cannot shed geography. As you will see in Chapters 2, 3 and 5, the spatial aspects of community are central to social welfare and crime control policy agendas and to 'bottom-up' local community activism.

Map of Multicultural London

(a) Hammersmith & Fulham
(b) Kensington & Chelsea
(c) Westminster

01 African London

Elephant & Castle (Southwark)
Hackney and Dalston (Hackney)
Leytonstone (Waltham Forest)
Peckham (Southwark)
Tottenham (Haringey)

02 Asian London

Brick Lane (Tower Hamlets)
Green St, Upton Park (Newham)
Southall (Ealing)
Tooting (Wandsworth)
Wembley (Brent)

03 Caribbean London

Brixton (Lambeth)
Hackney and Dalston (Hackney)
Harlesden (Brent)
Notting Hill (Kensington & Chelsea)

04 Chinese London

Chinatown (Westminster)
Colindale (Barnet)
Croydon (Croydon)

05 European London

Golborne Road (Kensington & Chelsea)
Soho (Westminster)
South Kensington (Kensington & Chelsea)
Stockwell (Lambeth)

06 Greek London

Haringey (Haringey)
Palmers Green (Enfield)
Newington Green (Islington)
Wood Green (Haringey)

07 Irish London

Camden Town (Camden)
Kilburn (Brent)
Queen's Park (Brent)
Willesden (Brent)

08 Japanese London

Finchley (Barnet)
Golders Green (Barnet)
Swiss Cottage (Camden)

09 Jewish London

Golders Green (Barnet)
Stamford Hill (Hackney)

10 Latin American London

Elephant & Castle (Southwark)
Finsbury Park (Haringey)

11 Middle Eastern London

Bayswater (Kensington & Chelsea)
Edgware Road (Westminster)
Shepherd s Bush (Hammersmith & Fulham)

12 Polish London

Hammersmith (Hammersmith & Fulham)
Kensington (Kensington & Chelsea)
Ealing (Ealing)

13 South East Asian London

Kingsland Road (Hackney)
Mare Street (Hackney)

14 Turkish London

Hackney and Dalston (Hackney)
Green Lanes/Turnpike Lane (Haringey)
Newington Green (Islington)
Stoke Newington (Hackney)

Figure 1.4
Greater London Authority's map of multicultural London

3.2 Communities as non-spatial sites of identity and culture

Moving on from the notion of community as being in and of a particular place, we now wish to suggest that community can be manifested *beyond* place and locality. People are able to experience bonds of belonging with others they will never meet or know, or with whom they will never directly socially interact. Thus, despite the absence of face-to-face bonds, people may still act or behave in ways that reflect a sense of community. An example of this can be seen in what happened following the earthquake in the Pakistan-governed area of Kashmir in 2005. The earthquake, in which an estimated 100,000 people died, received intense media coverage. In particular, British Muslims, who had familial and faith connections to the areas affected, organised an extensive relief operation that despatched supplies to Kashmir.

In this way, communities can be thought of as having meaning tied to identities other than place (Chapter 5 will examine in more detail how the notion of community can be mobilised independently of place). One of the key ways in which this understanding of communities has developed is through the concept of *diaspora*. 'Diaspora' comes from the Greek word for 'disperse'. The concept of diaspora has its origins in the forced exile of Jewish peoples, by the Roman Empire, from what is now Israel and Palestine. However, it is used increasingly by social theorists to explain how migrations have all resulted in the globally scattered relocation of populations away from original homelands.

These populations may have an ambivalent or hybrid attachment (which is often intensified by hostilities in receiving societies) to the nation states in which they have settled. Immediate and new generations of diasporic populations retain not only a sense of collective attachment to original homelands, but also a strong ethnic consciousness – again, the Kashmir earthquake example illustrates this. It is these features – collective memory, an idealised but long-left and perhaps never-visited 'homeland', a sense of ties to and recognition of unknown members of the same ethnic group – that constitute diasporic populations as communities. These are communities whose 'community-ness' is not based in a particular locality. This non-spatial sense of community and belonging is enhanced in contemporary settings by technological developments (the internet, satellite television, mobile phones), financial flows (migrants sending money 'back home') and geographical mobility (aided by cheap air travel). Increasingly, diasporic communities are multiply located – they are transnational, their bonds of community are imagined and they are rooted in an everyday geography, as the London map in Figure 1.4 shows.

This idea of imagined communities is an important one for us because it loosens the concept of community from the locality and allows it to work on a much larger level, as ways in which people connect, identify and interact with each other. It is by shifting communities away from locality and on to 'meaning' that we can understand the everyday usage of community in relation to such groupings as 'the disabled community'; 'the black community'; 'minority ethnic communities'; 'the Muslim community'; 'the lesbian and gay community'; 'the Gypsy Traveller community'. These categories of community, which are used regularly in political, policy and everyday discourses, are identity-based categories. It is important for us to note that while some people may claim to belong to these communities (and organise on that basis), other people are also assigned to such communities by policymakers, service deliverers and the media, rather than actively choosing to define themselves in such terms. One of the dangers of this process of assignment of groups of people to specific categories of community is the way in which it tends to homogenise the people deemed to belong to a particular community, thereby obscuring social diversity, social divisions and social differences within those categories.

Communities that are referenced through social and cultural identity may still have a relation to place. The social theorist Benedict Anderson (1991) has argued that 'the national community' – Britain, Mexico, Japan, Ghana, for example – is an imagined category. Nations are about a place and a territory – but not a territory that is necessarily geographically familiar to all those who are part of the national community. The national community is imagined because the vast majority of its members are, of course, not personally acquainted. As the chapters in this book demonstrate, identity and place interconnect in complex ways in local, regional, national and international contexts. The anthropologist Anthony Cohen (1987) has argued that understanding community as meaning – that is, of the mind – involves a dependency on symbols and practices around which people may hang their identity and community membership. Cohen argues that 'virtually anything can be grist to the symbolic mill' (Cohen, 1987, p. 117). These symbols (language, dress, diet, religion) and practices (rituals, customs, celebrations) change, and require interpretation to give them community meaning. In this way, community is not fixed and static but imprecise and open to interpretation. However, if such symbols are heavily or extensively invested with a particular meaning, this reinforces more fixed notions of community identity.

Activity 1.4

Think back to Activity 1.1 at the beginning of Section 2. How many of your definitions of community were based on identity and culture rather than on an actual place? What symbols or practices do you think you used to select some of your examples of communities?

Comment

The symbols used to define a community work because they mark out cultural and/or identity differences. Here we might include history, language, food, diet, dress, religion and faith-based customs. The everyday social practices and celebratory rituals associated with some of these symbols – sporting events, weddings, funerals, births, Christmas, Eid, Hanukkah, St Patrick's Day, Notting Hill Carnival, eisteddfods, fetes and melas – all emphasise distinct identity formations. Think back to Harry Bernstein's story and his description of the line of separation or boundaries between the residents on East Street. A number of commentators on community have argued that, more than anything, community signifies the separation or the boundaries in social relationships. It is this focus on community as boundary that we consider next.

3.3 Communities as boundaries and sites of conflict

You have seen how commentators such as Cohen (1987) have argued that communities do not exist in terms of structures or institutions, but in terms of meaning and culture. Communities of meaning require a range of symbols that can be interpreted, depending on an individual's relationship to those symbols, as definers of membership (or not) of particular communities. In effect, what these symbols do is construct boundaries. Communities are defined through difference and against one another. In other words, they are about those on the inside *and* those on the outside. Akhil Gupta and James Ferguson (1997, p. 3) argue that 'community is ... a categorical identity that is premised on various forms of exclusion and construction of otherness'. There are any number of examples for thinking of communities as sites of boundary assertion and conflict – for instance, the sectarian divisions in areas of cities such as Belfast, Liverpool and Glasgow. Religion is one axis of division; social and economic factors such as class, national identity and ethnicity are others. These lines of division and community affiliations are not necessarily permanent. They do and can shift and change. They can be fixed and hard and very visible, or they can be fluid and permeable and not particularly apparent. Community boundaries are drawn around identity and culture, as discussed in Section 3.2, but they often incorporate a spatial dimension. In Extract 1.4 we have included another example from the research carried out by Sarah Neal and Sue Walters, which illustrates a sense both of a community boundary and of threat in an everyday setting. In the extract, you will read a conversation from a focus group interview with young people involved in their local Young Farmers' Club, in which they are talking about their feelings regarding rural legislation introduced by what they see as urban-based planners.

Extract 1.4

Dan: There is no proper agriculture anymore

Molly: There's so many regulations now.

Annie: Since foot-and-mouth these people called English Nature sit in an office in London and my Dad always used quad bikes on the fell and they tell us we are not allowed to use them.

Richard: There are so many restrictions on things.

Annie: They don't understand that you have to

Molly: How are you going to get over

Annie: You can't walk around hundreds of miles.

Richard: Well, it's just typical of people in towns making decisions.

Molly: Exactly. They're all out of touch with the countryside.

Richard: People in towns make decisions for us.

Neal and Walters, 2007, p. 260

In this extract, it is possible to see a community boundary being asserted and a perception of the rural community being threatened by the interventions of urban outsiders who 'don't understand' rural communities, but who are nevertheless making decisions that impact negatively on rural practices.

In the examination, in later chapters of this book, of the ways in which community illuminates the entanglement between social and crime policy, the concept of community-as-boundaries is important. There is a contradiction between strong communities being seen, on the one hand, as desirable for social cohesion and, on the other, as a source of social problems. This contradiction is compounded, as Chapters 2 and 4 explore, by the ways in which community then becomes identified as the answer to social problems. Below are two examples of communities whose boundaries are problematically 'strong'.

The first example is from research into 'grassing' and cultures of loyalty and trust in a deprived area of Salford, by the criminologist Sandra Walklate and her colleagues, who found a correlation not between community breakdown and high crime rates, but rather, between high crime rates and strong senses of community. Established community bonds and kinship networks were effectively able to support 'criminal networks and subcultures' (cited in Young, 1999, p. 177).

Figure 1.5
Shameless and *The Sopranos*: television representations of communities with strong bonds

The second example relates to concern over strongly bounded communities, which have long been a central feature of the debates about contemporary multicultural societies. One of the most publicised and commented-on findings of the government inquiry into the urban unrest that took place in towns across northern England in the summer of 2001 was the extent of the boundaries between local white and Muslim communities living in towns such as Oldham, Bradford and Burnley (Cantle, 2001). The Cantle Report was particularly concerned with the extent to which local communities were, in effect, segregated and living 'parallel lives', and how, in such contexts, fear, mistrust and conflict were likely to threaten social cohesion and social order. The cultural segregation analysis of the social disorder in northern England has driven the multicultural social policy approach in the UK since 2001 (see also Chapter 5). This approach has shifted policy from an emphasis on the value of cultural diversity to an emphasis on community cohesion and integration.

In both these examples we can see that what some communities (are thought to) 'do' and 'not do' can be interpreted as highly problematic, socially divisive and a threat to social order. How communities behave and what communities do, don't do and can do has increasingly become a key driver in social and crime control policy approaches and interventions. This leads us to our fourth approach to understanding community.

3.4 Communities as sites of citizenship and governance

The example from the Cantle Report above referred to a discussion of the tensions caused by too strongly bounded communities. You saw how community was interpreted as a social problem. However, as you have also seen, social policy has argued not against community but, rather, for *more* community. Think back to Section 2 and the nationally sponsored community week recommended by the Commission on Integration and Cohesion, for example. A further example is the 2006 White Paper, *Strong and Prosperous Communities: The Local Government White Paper* (DCLG, 2006), the title of which reflects the White Paper's core theme that governments must think local and think community.

Some of the current political investment in the concept of community lies in its seeming ability to deliver social welfare, to foster people's social and civic participation and thereby also deliver on issues of social order and social inclusion. The relationship between community structures, institutions and values has been called 'civic communitarianism' (Delanty, 2003). Although some of the principles of civic communitarianism are not new and have long been part of political debates about citizenship and the relationship between individuals and society, what is more recent is the development of communitarianism as political projects in both the UK and the USA. We will consider the arguments of two examples of civic communitarianism: from the work of Robert Putnam and Amitai Etzioni.

Putman's book *Bowling Alone: The Collapse and Revival of American Community* (2000) contends that community is in decline, and that the activities that make up community and cement bonds of social trust and mutuality are less evident. For Putnam, the decline of people's civic engagement is a reflection of increasing social disconnection and low civic participation:

> In 1992 three quarters of the US workforce said that breakdown of community and selfishness were serious or extremely serious problems in America. In 1996 only 8% of all Americans said that

the honesty and integrity of the average American were improving compared to 50% who thought Americans were becoming less trustworthy. In several surveys in 1999 two thirds of Americans said that America's civic life had weakened in recent years; that social and moral values were higher when they were growing up and that American society was focused more on the individual than the community. More than 80% said there should be more emphasis on community even if it put more demands on individuals.

(Putnam, 2000, p. 25)

These are some of a range of statistics presented by Putnam to emphasise the public anxiety about the decline of community in the USA. He claims that the decline of community is multifactored and includes changing traditional family structures, suburbanisation, work patterns, television, and generational approaches. These have all played a part in breaking down social bonds, trust, volunteerism and engagement in social institutions. For Putnam, this is a decline in *social capital*, by which he means the individual and collective energies that are put into communities by their members, and which create local but powerful networks of trust and connectedness. He argues that communities with high levels of social capital mean healthier, better educated, more caring communities. (We will return to spend more time thinking about social capital in Section 4 and you will encounter this idea again in Chapter 2.)

Putnam has been criticised for an over-nostalgic and mythical vision of community, and for neglecting the divisions and conflicts that can also characterise it. He has also been criticised for placing too much responsibility on small-scale community organisations (such as parent–teacher associations) and activities to solve major social problems (Fine, 2001). These kinds of criticisms have also been made against the work of Amitai Etzioni.

Consider a very brief extract from Etzioni's book *The Spirit of Community* (1993). This extract is taken from a larger discussion in the book on how to explain rising crime rates in a high-income country such as the USA. In this extract you can see that Etzioni argues (unlike the study by Walklate et al., which we considered briefly in Section 3.3) that there is a correlation between high crime rates and weak community structures and, more importantly for Etzioni, weak relations *between* key community institutions:

The level of crime is deeply affected by the total community fabric. It is not enough for families to be strong or schools to be fine educational institutions and so on. To minimise crime all of these elements must reinforce one another. Thus in those parts of the country (and the world) where families are strong, schools teach moral values, communities are well intact and values command respect ... families, schools, communities – all the factors that go into making the moral infrastructure – come together to support moral conduct. In effect they work not merely or mainly to fight crime but to sustain civility and values in general. Prevention of crime is a bonus in a moral and civil society.

(Etzioni, 1993, p. 191)

Figure 1.6
Social capital: organised communities?

The social theorist Jock Young (1999, pp. 160–1) argues that Etzioni reduces explanations of crime to issues of social order. For Etzioni, a strong *system of interconnected* institutions leads to an absence of crime. Crime is the outcome of social disorder rather than a consequence of social injustice or socio-economic divisions. Community is identified here as the site that affirms social order, moral consensus and authority. The relationship between community and social order is examined in Chapter 3, but what is important to stress here is the impact that these versions of communitarianism have had on recent political thinking and policymaking. What we can see in these kinds of ideas about strong communities is the emphasis on *local* worlds and on the *moral consensus* of community, rather than national governments or the state, as the sites in which social care and social control or order are established and from which they emanate.

For both Putnam and Etzioni, strong communities mean strong states. In this way, we can see that, increasingly, the concept of community is becoming a part of contemporary thinking with regard to ways in which populations might be managed and their social needs and well-being facilitated. In the remainder of this section, it is this perspective on community – as an arena in or through which to *govern* populations – that we wish to consider.

One of the key social theorists associated with arguing that community can work as a site of governance is Nikolas Rose. Rose draws on the work of another social theorist, Michel Foucault. At the heart of Foucault's work (1991, 2001) is an argument that social control and power need to be understood not simply as working from the top down – that is, from ruler to subject – but as operating through more greatly dispersed and decentred routes involving numerous agents. These routes include the ways in which individuals internalise notions of behaviour and discipline themselves accordingly. For Rose, community can become one of those routes through which the behaviour or conduct of populations is regulated, and where people learn to regulate themselves. Think back, for example, to some of the earlier discussions in this chapter where we argued that community is a concept that has belonging at its heart – to belong requires a degree of conformity to the values and practices that define a community. For Rose, Putnam and Etzioni's concept of communitarianism represents attempts

> to regenerate and reactivate the ethical values that are now believed to regulate individual conduct and that help maintain order and obedience to law by binding individuals into shared moral norms and values; governing through the self steering forces of honour and shame, of propriety, obligation, trust, fidelity and commitment to others.
>
> (Rose, 2000, p. 324)

Community becomes governmental when it is the *instrument* through which governments focus their strategies for controlling and regulating social conduct *and* for developing non-state based strategies for meeting the welfare and social needs of individuals, families and particular populations. Rose argues that this represents a shift in welfare provision away from the state as a *central provider* to an emphasis on the state as a *decentred partner* that seeks to facilitate individuals, families and communities to be responsible, self-reliant and prudent, and 'to take upon themselves the responsibility for the security of their property, persons, families ... they must educate themselves with the assistance of experts and must actively engage in partnerships with expertise to maintain order and combat threats to individual and collective security' (Rose, 1999, p. 327).

It is possible to see some of this in such policy approaches as neighbourhood regeneration, antisocial behaviour strategies and community safety partnerships, all of which centre on ideas of multi-agency networks and community leaders. These types of policy formation will be the subject of examination in the chapters that you will go on to read in this book. Chapters 2, 3 and 4 will take you back to the work of Rose as they examine the relationship between communities and policymaking, social order and crime prevention.

This section has taken you through four different but connected approaches to community: community as understood through space and face-to-face interaction; community as understood through identity formations and imagined connections; community as a boundary that exists only because it is able to include some and exclude others; and community as a way in which populations and their social needs and behaviours can be governed and managed. These four approaches are summarised in Table 1.2. Each is important for us in thinking through the entanglements of social welfare and crime control policy. We do not want to discount any of the approaches or put them into any hierarchical order. Rather, we would like to encourage you to keep all four in mind as you read through this book, and to think about the different ways in which community works in everyday, political and policy contexts.

Table 1.2 Four approaches to defining community

Approaches	Themes	Welfare	Crime	Thinkers
Community as a spatial concept	Face-to-face interaction in locality/place	Safe places Care Trust	Problem places	Tönnies Chicago School
Community as non-spatial sites of identity and culture	Community formed through identity and imagined connections	Well-being Belonging Connectedness	Social exclusions Social disorders	Anderson Cohen
Community as boundaries and sites of conflict	Community as inclusion and exclusion	Social cohesion	Social divisions Social inequalities	Gupta and Ferguson Cantle
Communities as sites of citizenship and governance	Community as political investment and regulation	Social bonds Civic participation	Regulation Discipline Maintenance of order	Putnam Etzioni Rose

In this section we have drawn on empirical social research, policy reports and academic argument to illustrate the meanings of the approaches to community. Our main concern in using this range of data is to stress the widespread and diverse engagement with the concept of community.

4 Communities and the concept of social capital

We have discussed the ways in which the concept of community can be used to stand in for and create a sense of social cohesion, togetherness and shared attitudes. In the previous section, we began to discuss how an increasingly influential way of thinking about these values is through the idea of social capital. At its most basic level, social capital refers to trust and connectedness between people, and the strong social networks and resources that develop from this.

Although social capital has an increasing presence in academic, policy and political contexts, it is not a new concept. As Rose (2000) reminds us, ideas of self-reliance, responsibility and prudence were seen in the nineteenth and early twentieth centuries as the basis for providing for individual and social well-being. It has been the widespread *re-emergence* of these ideas – bundled within the language of social capital – that has been significant. The appeal of social capital, like that of its close relation, community, lies in the fact that it is not self-evident, but is highly flexible, has a wide applicability and emphasises individual-, family- and community-produced resources. Like community, social capital is one of the few social science concepts that have successfully travelled out of academic discourses and into everyday, political and policymaking arenas. From global to local and from macro- to micro-level policymaking contexts, social capital is also proving to be a key policy driver. It has informed the policy thinking of national governments, including in the UK and the USA, as well as transnational organisations such as the World Bank and the OECD (Organisation for Economic Co-operation and Development). In relation to educational attainment and outcomes, urban social policy, social development in developing countries, and crime prevention and control, social capital, as a converging discourse with community, is being mobilised both as a way of describing and explaining 'problems' and as a prescription for addressing them.

For Putnam (2000), social capital provides a way of making sense of social change and the apparent growth of 'moods' of insecurity, uncertainty, fear and precariousness (see **Cochrane and Talbot, 2008**). But more importantly it offers a way of renewing society on the basis of a 'revival' of community. While it reflects longer existing traditions in social and political thought, its reincarnation in the late 1990s and early 2000s is in part explained by the different ways in which it meets with trends and shifts in policymaking. In particular, the concept of social capital accompanies a shift in focus towards reinvigorating civic participation and the local in relation to governance and policy delivery. In this respect, it is distinct from political traditions that prioritise the role either of the state or of the individual. Increased levels of local civic engagement and involvement enhance a sense of community and well-being and contribute to greater feelings of safety, stability and belonging in a world that is seen as more insecure, uncertain and risky (see Chapters 2 and 4).

Although social capital certainly does hold appeal, with its emphasis on 'people power' and social trust, there are nevertheless a number of criticisms of it. A key concern is that social capital has been associated with a nostalgic vision of a 1950s world of social clubs and community organisations, which sits at odds with the social divisions and practices of exclusion that defined societies in the global North and West at that time. Indeed, the processes of social capital can be seen to be contributing directly to practices of exclusion. We consider this criticism in relation to sociologist Sergio Chávez's (2005) study of the local community of Yodoy, a small rural town in California.

Activity 1.5

Read the short extract from Chávez's article, which is reproduced as Extract 1.5. What does it tell us about community and social capital? Try to pick out examples of both as you read the extract.

Extract 1.5

Many Mexican residents asserted that they were willing to become part of formal social organizations, but there were barriers that prevented them from exercising their rights as community citizens. Additionally, recent Mexican immigrants were less likely to be involved in formal social organizations because of their undocumented status, lack of English competency or simply because these organizations did not cater to their needs. Nonetheless, community for Mexicans was constructed through participation in an organization that they saw as important to their well-being in U.S. society.

...

In my observations at an English-as-a-second language night class for immigrants, I also found that low-income Mexican women discussed state and local politics; taught each other the ins and outs of social services agencies; and created networks to strategize ways to help raise money in the school. Mexicans were also actively involved in the maintenance of the local park where they held soccer tournaments ...

While I observed these instances of community making, almost no [white] resident I spoke with considered Mexicans as contributing members of the town [... rather] Mexicans were [seen as] creating community in ways that promoted their ethnic and class differences which some white residents saw as threatening to the agrarian culture of the town and to American values.

Chávez, 2005, pp. 322, 323

Comment

You may have picked up on the desire for Mexican residents to be part of communities – the town community, the migratory Mexican community. You may also have identified the way in which the Mexican migrants, particularly women, used their social networks to help other Mexicans in Yodoy – the English language classes, for example. You may have noted the white residents' hostility to the town's Mexican residents despite their community work. Local white residents interpreted this community work not as neighbourly and civic, but the opposite – as threatening traditional (white American) Yodoy values. In this study, activities associated with social capital do not produce an integrated and trustful local community.

Critics have questioned the extent to which social capital can be effective without reference to broader social and economic divisions. Again, the study by Chávez is interesting because it illuminates the limits of social capital and illustrates the ways in which social capital can work in communities of need, which draw on it as a basis for survival and making claims on citizenship (Chapters 4 and 5 examine this in more detail). This is not to argue against social capital, but to suggest that it is used with some caution.

The need for a cautious approach is further emphasised when we consider the ways in which evidence is drawn on in social capital debates. Putnam (2000) uses different definitions of social capital in his studies, including 'civic virtue' and 'connections between people', so we may not be clear about exactly what it is that is being looked for. From these definitions we can see that Putnam is making major moral and political claims about *qualitative* changes – that there is a loss of community, a breakdown in social trust – but that he sees these changes as *quantifiable* – as measurable. For him, participation in community associations and activities (e.g. tenpin bowling leagues and picnics) is an important indicator of civic engagement. However, *which* associations and activities count as accurate measures of civic engagement? Putnam is criticised for focusing too much on 'mainstream' kinds of civic activity (Edwards et al., 2007). As Chávez's research shows, different members of the same community can be excluded from 'mainstream' community activities and may demonstrate alternative patterns of networking that are not equally valued.

We have spent some time in this section discussing the concept of social capital, what it is and why it has been problematic. We have indicated that people do indeed draw on and organise themselves through the resources and skills they are able to generate and then share. However, the extent to which social capital has impacted on a range of policymaking worlds might be interpreted as part of the shift in social welfare and crime control policy away from wider social and economic structures and processes and towards making individuals, families and communities responsible for their own welfare and life situations. Research evidence can shed light on the idea of social capital, but exactly how it is most effectively measured and assessed presents a range of challenges (see Chapter 5).

5   The structure of *Community: Welfare, Crime and Society*

In the last part of this chapter, we want to outline briefly how each of the following chapters picks up from what we have discussed here, and variously develops these early accounts of, and questions about, community and its relation to social and crime policy.

Chapter 2 takes up the question that we have raised regarding why community has become a key focus in social policy. Using case study examples, Chapter 2 investigates the way in which community has offered policymakers an arena in which to formulate and deliver social welfare and crime control policies.

Chapter 3 develops core themes that have been introduced in this first chapter. It examines the relationship between notions of community, social change and social order, and looks at this in the contexts of the rural community, the working-class community, colonial governance and the contemporary community of London's East End.

Chapter 4 picks up from some of our discussion in Sections 3.4 and 4 in the present chapter, concerning the concept of governance or management of populations. Developing this discussion, Chapter 4 makes an explicit return to the connections between policy and community through a detailed focus on the way in which community has been central to policy development and political thinking in relation to crime prevention and public safety.

Chapter 5 goes on to look at community from a different position. It explores how community can operate from 'below' – at an everyday grass-roots level. Chapter 5 is interested in how the notion of community is used by people as a way to connect with and support other people (family, neighbours, friends) and as a vehicle through which to organise, lobby and demand social goods and resources.

Each of the chapters draws on and uses case study examples in its discussion. Each chapter also provides a range of evidence and explores the relationship between community as a social science concept, evidence about community and the impact and incorporation of these into a range of local, regional, national and international policy agendas.

Chapter 6 concludes the book. It returns to the questions and themes we have raised here in Chapter 1, and reflects on how the book as a whole has explored these. It also considers the ways in which theory, evidence and policymaking converge in the category of 'community'.

6   Review

We have travelled a considerable distance from our opening question as to why understanding community can provide a route into examining the entanglements between social welfare and crime control policies. We have argued that community offers an effective key for unlocking some of the aspects of these entanglements because:

- community stands as 'shorthand' for 'good social relations', social belonging and stability

- community has been associated with explanations of social disorder and conflict and used to categorise social problems and 'problem populations'

- community is being mobilised increasingly as a political and policy 'answer' for addressing and managing social problems and for developing social responsibility for welfare and security.

In this chapter we have urged you to approach the concept of community with care. The points above alert us to the fact that community is a concept that represents multiple and often convergent meanings. Section 2 examined the range of definitions and ways in which community is interpreted. Section 3 outlined the ways in which community has been approached within academic debates. Although we organised these into four main approaches, the chapter has stressed that these approaches should not be seen as completely separate: they can and do intersect with and sustain each other. Some of this relationality can be seen in the concept of social capital, which we discussed in

Section 4. We argued that community and social capital are concepts that have impacted on policy and political agendas, and have been promoted as ways in which people may be managed and/or may manage themselves. These discussions will be explored further in the following chapters. Finally, evidence has been a key element of the chapter. You have encountered a range of both quantitative and qualitative data through the interview findings, statistics, observations and policy texts that have been incorporated. In threading evidence through the chapter in this way, we hope that we have begun to enable you to see a set of connections between social science concepts, social science research, political agendas and policy development.

Further reading

There are numerous books and studies devoted to an exploration of different aspects of 'community'. A good introductory overview is provided by Graham Day in *Community and Everyday Life* (2006, Routledge). Vered Amit and Nigel Rapport's *The Trouble with Community* (2002, Pluto) is a co-authored conversation between two anthropologists, which usefully addresses the ways in which community has been conceptualised and practised in the contemporary world. In particular, it is concerned with the tensions between collective and fragmented identities and the impact of such tensions on current social relations. John Field's *Social Capital* (2002, Routledge) provides an accessible overview of many of the different debates that surround the notion of social capital, as well as considering how the idea has come to be influential in policymaking at national and global levels.

References

Amit, V. and Rapport, N. (2002) *The Trouble with Community*, London, Pluto.

Anderson, B. (1991) *Imagined Communities*, London, Verso.

Bauman, Z. (2001) *Community*, London, Polity Press.

Bell, C. and Newby, H. (1971) *Community Studies*, London, Unwin.

Bernstein, H. (2007) *The Invisible Wall*, London, Hutchinson.

Cantle, T. (2001) *Community Cohesion: A Report of the Independent Review Team*, London, Home Office.

Chávez, S. (2005) 'Community, ethnicity and class in a changing rural California town', *Rural Sociology*, vol. 70, no. 3, pp. 314–35.

Cochrane, A. and Talbot, D. (eds) (2008) *Security: Welfare, Crime and Society*, Maidenhead, Open University Press/Milton Keynes, The Open University.

Cohen, A. (1987) *The Symbolic Construction of Community*, London, Sage.

Commission on Integration and Cohesion (2007) *Final Report: Our Shared Future*, London, Commission on Integration and Cohesion.

Cresswell, T. (2004) *Place: A Short Introduction*, London, Blackwell.

Delanty, G. (2003) *Community,* London, Routledge.

Department for Communities and Local Government (DCLG) (2006) *Strong and Prosperous Communities: The Local Government White Paper*, Cm 6939-I-II, London, The Stationery Office.

Edwards, R., Franklin, J. and Holland, J. (eds) (2007) *Assessing Social Capital: Concept, Policy and Practice*, Cambridge, Cambridge Scholars Publishing.

Etzioni, A. (1993) *The Spirit of Community: Rights, Responsibilities, and the Communitarian Agenda*, New York, Crown Publishing.

Fine, B. (2001) *Social Capital Versus Social Theory*, London, Routledge.

Foucault, M. (1991) *Discipline and Punish: The Birth of the Prison*, London, Penguin Social Sciences.

Foucault, M. (2001) *Madness and Civilization*, London, Routledge.

Gupta, A. and Ferguson, J. (eds) (1997) *Culture, Power, Place: Explorations in Critical Anthropology*, Durham, NC, Duke University Press.

McCarthy, J.R. (2008) 'Security, insecurity and family lives' in Cochrane, A. and Talbot, D. (eds) (2008) *Security: Welfare, Crime and Society*, Maidenhead, Open University Press/Milton Keynes, The Open University.

Massey, D. (1994) *Space, Place and Gender*, Minnesota, MN, University of Minnesota Press.

Neal, S. and Walters, S. (2006) 'Strangers asking strange questions? A methodological narrative of researching belonging and identity in English rural communities', *Journal of Rural Studies*, vol. 22, no. 2, pp. 177–89.

Neal, S. and Walters, S. (2007) '"You can get away with loads because there's no one here": discourses of regulation and non-regulation in English rural spaces', *GeoForum*, vol. 38, no. 2, pp. 252–75.

Neal, S. and Walters, S. (2008) 'Rural be/longing and rural social organizations: conviviality and community-making in the English countryside', *Sociology*, vol. 42, no. 2, pp. 279–97.

Park, R. (1915) 'The city: suggestions for the investigation of human behavior in the city', *American Journal of Sociology*, vol. 20, no. 5, pp. 577–612.

Pilkington, E. (2007) 'Divided loyalties', *The Guardian*, 12 February, pp. 12–13; also available online at http://books.guardian.co.uk/departments/politicsphilosophyandsociety/story/0,,2011169,00.html (Accessed 26 March 2008).

Putnam, R.D. (2000) *Bowling Alone: The Collapse and Revival of American Community*, New York, Simon & Schuster.

Rose, N. (1999) *Powers of Freedom*, Cambridge, Cambridge University Press.

Rose, N. (2000) 'Government and control', *British Journal of Criminology*, vol. 40, no. 2, pp. 321–39.

Savage, M., Bagnall, G. and Longhurst, B. (2005) *Globalisation and Belonging*, London, Sage.

Stacey, M. (1969) 'The myth of community studies', *British Journal of Sociology*, vol. 20, no. 2, pp. 134–47.

Tönnies, F. (1963) *Community and Society*, New York, Harper Row.

Young, J. (1999) *The Exclusive Society*, London, Sage.

Young, M. and Willmott, P. (1957) *Family and Kinship in East London*, Harmondsworth, Penguin.

Chapter 2
Community and policymaking

Allan Cochrane and Janet Newman

Contents

1   Introduction

In the previous chapter, you were introduced to ways of thinking about and understanding the notion of 'community', and, in particular, the complex and contested ways in which it is mobilised in the fields of welfare and crime control policy. In this chapter, we take that discussion further by focusing specifically on the ways in which 'community' has been interpreted as an object of and frame for social policy and crime management interventions. In this context, communities have been understood in a range of overlapping and sometimes contradictory ways: as sites in which social problems are clustered; as potential agents of social improvement and renewal; and, more pragmatically, as alternatives to institutionally based care and incarceration.

The aims of this chapter are to:

■ clarify how notions of community have been drawn on in policy development

■ explore, in particular, the ways in which community has become a key focus of policies aiming to control antisocial behaviour

■ identify some of the possibilities and limitations of community-based policy

■ reflect on the ways in which different forms of evidence may be used to interpret the nature and impact of public policy.

Sections 2, 3 and 4 explore each of the main issues in turn, while Section 5 draws out broad conclusions. Throughout the chapter, we consider the way in which a range of evidence may be used to explore how community is understood in the process of policymaking, and actively mobilised in the process of implementation.

2   Community as the focus of state action and intervention

Activity 2.1

To start our discussion, we want to look at the ways in which notions of community are used in the public services and the voluntary sector. The examples in Figure 2.1 were all taken from job advertisements published in the UK: you could find other examples for yourself. We have edited them to clarify some of the underlying principles, and have anonymised them because we believe that general points can be drawn without identifying the particular agencies (or places) involved. As you look at the examples we offer, we would like you to think about:

■ how the language of community is being used – what it seems to mean (think about the kinds of place, the kinds of values, and the sorts of relationships that are assumed)

■ how community is mobilised in policy – what are the policy goals to which each job might be linked? Of course, you won't know the detail of particular policies, but you might think about what the person who fills the job would be asked to do, and how this might contribute to achieving goals linked to welfare and/or crime control.

1   *Service Manager, Older People and People with Physical and Sensory Impairments.* 'With a brand new Adult Community Care Department, a new Director and fresh vision already established … We want to deliver a brighter service for everyone in our community. We want to make a real difference to the lives of the people we work with.'

2   **Community Safeguarding and Intervention.** '*A new and vibrant service dedicated to safeguarding children in the community … a chance to be at the forefront of "making a difference" for children and their families … working closely with our Adolescent Support Team and other partners in the community to provide family support that is sensitive to the needs of our vibrant and multicultural community.*'

3   *Community Protection: City Guardian.* 'Join us and you will act as a constant, reassuring presence within the community, reducing crime and the fear of crime throughout your work. We are looking for people who like everyday life to be different and who want to make a difference to communities, make the environment better, and who want to work to reduce crime and make people feel safer.'

4   *Service Manager, Community Development.* 'We want all our communities to thrive, now and in the future. You could play a major part in achieving this … You will be responsible for community engagement and community safety. You will have day-to-day responsibility for managing sports and arts development, voluntary sector support and community grants, community transport, environmental and health initiatives.'

5   ***Community Empowerment Network Coordinator.*** 'Administering the Community Empowerment Network which helps voluntary and community sector organisations through grants and programmes, you will drive forward local people's involvement in key decision-making through networking at all levels … You will develop local leaders in the community, broker new partnerships and support local community projects and networks.'

Figure 2.1
Serving the community

Comment

These brief extracts suggest some of the rich diversity of the roles that community has come to play in social and public policy. Reflecting on the first of the questions set out at the beginning of this exercise – 'how the language of community is being used' – we can see that in some cases it denotes particular *people*, whereas in others it suggests a particular *place*. Extract 1, for example, clearly refers to particular categories of person – adults in need, particularly older people and people with physical or sensory impairments – as 'our community'; that is, the people to whom services are being delivered. Extract 2 refers to 'children in the community', again implying a category of person: in this case, a category of person in need of safeguarding and protection, rather than the recipient of particular 'services'. Extracts 3, 4 and 5, by contrast, refer to 'local community' or 'local people' and call on a broad understanding of community as those living in a particular locality (probably defined by local authority boundaries). Many policy interventions are narrowly targeted on a defined place: usually an area with a high crime rate, or a neighbourhood or estate facing particular challenges of deprivation or disadvantage that policy interventions seek to overcome. In practice, then, communities as 'kinds of people' and as 'kinds of place' are collapsed into each other, with assumptions that 'problem people' often live in 'problem places' (**Mooney, 2008**).

However, community as place also has positive associations: the reference to 'community care' in Extract 1, while targeted at a particular group, denotes personalised support which is intended to enable members of the group to remain in the 'community'; that is, in familiar surroundings and close to existing social networks. We can look at how these positive associations of community are invoked in the language of the advertisements, with the aim of the jobs concerned being associated with making communities feel 'safe and supported' (Extract 2), making people feel 'safer' (Extract 3), and working towards communities that 'will thrive' (Extract 4) and towards the 'empowerment' of communities (Extract 5).

This begins to take us towards the second question posed above, which is about how community and policy are linked (see also Chapter 4). Here we want to make four points. *First*, community often appears to be used in policy discussion as *a response to criticisms of (welfare) state intervention for delivering services from the top down*: government delivering services *to* people or *for* people, rather than *with* people. It has been argued that top-down approaches may encourage the development of a dependency culture; that is, one in which poor and disadvantaged people simply rely on state assistance instead of being enabled to act independently. But such approaches have also been criticised on the grounds that they fail to take into account what people (whether relabelled users, consumers or customers) actually want. This implies looking for means of delivering policy in different ways, perhaps through the range of 'partnerships' mentioned in the advertisements. In many countries, responses to the 'crisis' of the welfare state (discussed by **Clarke, 2008**) have meant that services that were previously provided directly by the state have been privatised, contracted out or made the responsibility of 'families and communities', although communities have long been, to some extent, seen as a site for policy delivery (a point to which we will return later in Section 4). Community care, the policy context which underlies Extract 1, was designed explicitly to shift services from a model of state-provided residential care to one in which people are enabled to stay in their own homes with support from care services (usually provided by the voluntary sector or private companies) and from informal carers (family members, children, neighbours, friends). This was not simply a case of the state abandoning people in need. In the UK, the National Health Service and Community Care Act 1990 was, in part, a response to pressure from a number of different social movements (e.g. those of disabled people) that presented sharp criticisms of the tradition of institutional care.

Community, in this context, takes on a particular value as an *alternative to direct state provision* – and an alternative that is held to be better than the state in a number of respects. It is said to be better in that people are freed up from the paternalism of state institutions. It may also be more cost-effective, pushing responsibility back on to people to care for themselves and others, rather than expecting the state to provide. Of course, shifting responsibility for social provision from the state to communities, in their different forms, may leave some vulnerable people without any form of provision. It may also put pressure on voluntary and community-based organisations, leaving the sector overburdened and under-resourced. But community as the site and focus of policy remains very attractive: 'community' suggests something altogether warmer, more human and more personally engaging than 'state'.

The *second* way in which community and policy are linked, then, draws on the positive images of community traced in Chapter 1 of this book. These positive features create *a resource on which policymakers can draw*. We can see this clearly in Extracts 4 and 5. Here, community engagement and networking are understood to offer a more direct means of (two-way) communication between policymaker and service user than traditional approaches.

Some of these different features of community as a resource that can be mobilised in policy come together in the example of community policing, the principles of which find some expression in Extract 3. This can be interpreted as an indication both of *where* policing takes place (in 'communities'), and of *how* it takes – or should take – place (in collaboration with 'communities'). (Some of the issues relating to the role of 'communities' in delivering forms of security are discussed by **Cochrane and Talbot, 2008a; Jewkes, 2008**; Chapter 4 in this volume.) For example, community policing approaches draw on the notion of community in two distinct ways: in terms of the involvement and engagement of people (possibly by interest or identity as much as place) at different levels, and in terms of what has also been described as 'neighbourhood policing' (focused quite specifically on particular local areas) (Myhill, 2006).

Third, associated with these shifts is a rather different meaning of community, in which communities – in all the different forms highlighted in Chapter 1 – are being asked to be *partners in the delivery of policy*, doing work on behalf of themselves and others, and, in the process, helping to deliver key policy goals. This is sometimes identified as a process of co-production; that is, the notion that citizens should be directly involved in the delivery of services because their participation is so crucial in determining the policy outcomes that are sought. We can see this in the long list of responsibilities that the post holder in Extract 4 is asked to take on. In order to overcome inequality and disadvantage, this person has to draw on the community itself as a partner in community safety initiatives, in delivering community transport services, in implementing policies on community health and environmental issues, or in shaping a community leisure policy. The image here is of a very busy community, with the state – and state professionals – facilitating and enabling, but with responsibility for delivering policy goals shared between government, the voluntary and community sector and citizens themselves.

Many of the jobs in the five advertisements suggest how working in the community has come to mean working in partnership and drawing directly on the strengths of a 'vibrant' community, in some cases collaborating in the delivery of services. From this perspective, 'community leaders' have a particularly important role to play in this context, and government agencies – and voluntary organisations – may have to 'develop' them. The extent to which it has become commonplace to speak of the voluntary and community sector is particularly significant because of the way in which it implies the existence of appropriate partners capable of developing and delivering a range of services, as well as appearing to provide a ready-made set of institutions with which to undertake consultation and 'engagement'.

The *final* meaning of community mobilised in policy, with which we deal here, presents a rather more negative image. Here the community – either as place, or as group of people, or some mix of the two – is viewed as somehow deficient: as lacking skills and confidence, and as not having sufficient 'social capital' to solve its own problems (see Chapter 1). *Policy interventions designed to build and sustain community* are viewed as necessary to foster the connections and relationships, the skills and commitments that will enable communities to become more active. In this way, it is believed, communities might be able to take on a kind of partnership with government agencies to address problems of social inclusion and social cohesion, welfare and crime control. Although not explicitly stated in the extracts, elements of this approach are implicit in the emphasis on community participation, community development and community empowerment. The discussion of community protection in Extract 3 raises similar questions, since what is implied is that a dedicated officer is required to enable the community to find ways of challenging crime and criminal behaviour.

We will have more to say about this negative view of some communities later in the chapter. Here we want to conclude this section by looking across these different relationships between community and policy. The first general point is to note how popular community seems to have become as a means of generating social well-being and social cohesion in the context of concerns about rising crime, problems of inequality and deprivation, and social isolation. A positive image of community is often mobilised to offer a vision of what might be possible – not only something to which people might aspire, but also a moral vision of how they ought to behave. So, for example, one report encourages us to 'Imagine the open communities of 2020':

> thriving and prosperous places where people from all different backgrounds are equal, and where everyone matters – whether old or young, settled or new, Black or White. There are local places where all groups feel that they are treated fairly, and that they have a responsibility to others that transcends the differences between them. Places where people are not fearful of meeting their neighbours, and where they don't see individual differences as a barrier to the success of the whole community.
>
> ...
>
> Imagine places where people are confident about change and the benefits it brings, who are not threatened by others, and who are able to welcome newcomers and offer them the support they need. Where people themselves are the catalysts for change in their local communities – working to bridge the gaps between groups, and to

mediate through tensions and conflicts. Where people recognise that while there will always be difference, it need not always be divisive.

(Commission on Integration and Cohesion, 2007, p. 2)

Figure 2.2
Celebrating
community: the Luton
carnival, 1993;
a Carnival Queen

This positive image of community is taken from a report, commissioned by the UK Government, on how to bring about greater social integration and cohesion (see also Chapter 1). These terms register a shift in what 'welfare' has come to mean in much contemporary social policy. The word 'welfare' itself, as we noted above, has come to have rather negative associations, at the same time that the state – or the public sector – has come to play a reduced role in the provision of benefits and services to those in need. However, this does not necessarily mean a reduced role for governing agencies – rather, their role has expanded to include a concern with questions of how to bring about cohesive, integrated societies (see, for example, **Clarke, 2008**). Community, in this context, is viewed as a means of building a sense of belonging and togetherness in the face of fears about the consequences of social fragmentation and division.

The second general point we want to make builds on the first and concerns the 'community puzzle' – how is it that community is both a 'golden panacea' for the resolution of social ills, yet also the site of social problems? The 'problem populations' at which policy is often directed (**Mooney, 2008**) are frequently viewed in terms of particular 'communities' whose problems are reproduced; for example, as 'deprived' children become 'antisocial' youth, or as 'socially excluded' families perpetuate cycles of poverty. Attachment and identification with the 'wrong' values, in the 'wrong' communities, is, then, a source of social problems. Yet the answer to these problems appears to be *more* or *better* community. Community, by strengthening networks and fostering new kinds of social capital, is viewed here as a means of generating entrepreneurialism and social dynamism, not just belonging. This reminds us that community is a highly slippery concept capable of being attached to rather different political and social projects. We have to pay attention, then, to the ways in which the concept of community is 'filled up' in particular policy initiatives in particular sites.

3 Community and the management of social disorder

As you have seen, community is understood in a wide range of ways in framing policy intervention. Other interpretations could be added: faith communities, the business community, professional communities, communities of identity and 'race' (some of which stretch across national boundaries in what have been called diasporic communities), national communities, communities of nations, the international community, and so on. Particular policy developments may seek to engage with one or other, and sometimes several, of these, representing, reflecting or appealing to them and their interests. As Chapter 1 suggests, the 'community' is an almost taken-for-granted reference in political and popular discussion.

Here, however, we want to focus in detail on one particular set of policy developments that start from place- or neighbourhood-based understandings of community. Our aim is to explore the entanglements of welfare and crime control policy with the help of this focus, as reflected in community as a site of popular involvement and self-help, as well as an object of policing and control.

It is in this context that some of the most powerful and contradictory images of community come together. On the one hand, the downward spiral into crime and disorder is associated with particular communities in which 'Serious crime, violence and, in some places, racial conflict, become common currency' (Johnstone, 2004, p. 78). Yet at the same time, community appears to offer a way forward in the development of crime control policies that construct neighbourhoods as 'moral spaces' within which antisocial behaviour can be reduced through a process of social renewal (Whitehead, 2004, p. 63). Within the framing concept of 'community', it becomes possible to identify both the source of problems and the means of solving them. 'Proper' communities deliver solutions, whereas 'dysfunctional' communities work to reinforce and reproduce failure.

In this section, we introduce you to some examples of social science research on the impact of 'antisocial behaviour' policies in specific neighbourhoods. We focus on these antisocial behaviour policies as a form of community-based intervention that differs markedly from some of the other policies concerned with crime control and criminal justice; for example, those that deliver custodial sentences (see also **Fergusson and Muncie, 2008**; Chapter 4 in this volume). We have organised our discussion of this issue around activities that draw on research which looked at a series of different local interventions around curbing antisocial behaviour in the early twenty-first century. The research was conducted in England and Wales by a group of researchers at the University of Birmingham (Marian Barnes, Kathryn Farrow, Paul Mason, David Prior and Basia Spalek) and involved three distinct pieces of research. The first (Prior, 2006) focused on intervention aimed at changing the behaviour of families or individuals whose persistent antisocial behaviour meant that they were threatened with eviction from social housing (i.e. housing provided by a local authority or housing association). The second piece of research (Edwards et al., 2006) was an evaluation of an initiative – the Children's Fund – targeted at children in England and Wales, aged 5–13 years, who were considered at risk of social exclusion. The third (Prior et al., 2006) explored the relationship between action taken to tackle antisocial behaviour and that aiming to promote civil renewal in one urban area. The discussion that follows draws on an overview of the research projects (Prior, 2007).

Activity 2.2

The research to which Extract 2.1 relates looked at the work of one local project whose aim was to reduce levels of antisocial behaviour among tenants of social housing in a particular area. Enforcement strategies (to which reference is made in the first paragraph of the extract) are those that respond to particular acts of antisocial behaviour with sanctions of one sort or another (such as restrictions on the movement of individuals or groups).

Read through Extract 2.1. As you do so, try to identify:

■ the main principles underlying the crime control strategy being adopted

■ how the 'community' within which the tenants live is understood.

Extract 2.1

The strategy in play here was a distinctive one of *promoting behavioural change*. This goes beyond an enforcement strategy's core aim of putting a stop to specific episodes of anti-social behaviour, rather it seeks lasting change in the general attitudes and behaviours of individuals or families in their ongoing relationships with others. ...

A key initial task of project workers is to encourage the tenant to agree and sign up to a 'contract' setting out a programme of work to address their anti-social behaviour, with specific objectives and targets set out over a specified time period.

...

However, research into this project ... showed entrenched patterns of dysfunctional family life. Most tenants were single mothers and were unemployed, drug and alcohol misuse and diagnosed mental health problems were common, a number of families had significant debt problems, and children were often recorded as truanting or showing poor school performance. ... In many instances members of the household already had a history of court appearances, including criminal convictions and receipt of ASBOs [Anti-social Behaviour Orders] and injunctions: the imprint of earlier failed enforcement strategies was visible in the records of these people's lives. All of this suggested a paradox for the project, in that the technology of the contract typically required a level of discipline and organization on the part of tenants and family members that was precisely what these individuals and families evidently lacked. ... Acquiring basic skills of parenting or the techniques of anger management, and having both the courage and determination to try using them, was for many an even more remote possibility.

The result was a high level of 'drop out' from the project.

Prior, 2007, pp. 11, 12–13

Comment

This research takes us back to the idea of community as problem; that is, of particular communities as sites in which social problems (and 'problem people') are condensed (it also draws attention to the role of families in this process – see **McCarthy, 2008**). But it also opens up a different question about the relationship between enforcement and preventative strategies. Here the suggestion is that previous enforcement strategies – resulting in court appearances, convictions, ASBOs and injunctions – had had a limiting effect on the capacity for preventative strategies to succeed. The extract highlights the tension between supportive and disciplinary forms of intervention in the management of antisocial behaviour (see also **Cochrane and Talbot, 2008a**). The families and individuals here are presented in terms of a series of deficits (e.g. lack of 'discipline and organization'), which is consistent with an approach that would highlight the lack of community-based social capital (see Chapter 1).

Figure 2.3
Professionals engaging with the community

Activity 2.3

In the next extract, the focus is on a Children's Fund partnership in a metropolitan authority in the north of England (Mason and Prior, 2006; see also Edwards et al., 2006). Children's Fund initiatives are resourced centrally but planned and delivered through local partnerships. Twenty-five per cent of the budget for each local programme has to be allocated to preventing children from becoming involved in crime and antisocial behaviour.

When reading Extract 2.2:

■ try to identify the differences between the policy approach adopted here and the strategy discussed in the previous activity

■ think about the relationship between 'welfare' and 'crime control', and how this relationship takes different forms in different policy programmes.

Extract 2.2

... [T]he intervention strategies developed and implemented indicated a more complex and multi-dimensional approach to responding to the needs and risks faced by children in the local area. This approach arose out of the broad understandings of 'prevention' and 'risk' that were adopted by the programme. The programme was not primarily concerned with preventing instances of crime and anti-social behaviour by intervening directly to influence individual children's behaviour through use of legal powers (the 'enforcement' strategy), but with the need to prevent children experiencing a range of damaging impacts as a result of a cluster of risk factors, of which involvement in crime and anti-social behaviour was just one possible impact. Exposure of children to the risks of becoming involved in crime and anti-social behaviour was viewed as an aspect of social exclusion; the strategy became one of preventing children's social exclusion as the most effective means of preventing their involvement in crime and anti-social behaviour.

The strategic concern with social exclusion meant that the programme was potentially concerned with a wide range of policies, services and agencies ...

...

These initiatives were based on assumed links between, on the one hand, the provision of leisure and cultural activities, skills and education-orientated work, and different types of support for children and families, and on the other hand the risk of involvement in crime and risk-taking behaviour. For example, in one large city neighbourhood, services provided structured out-of-school and supplementary learning, holiday and Saturday activities for children and families, and home–school liaison. All involved in the services made reference to the links between enabling children and young people to engage in constructive activities, gain new skills, raise their confidence, and raise their educational engagement and achievement, and to reductions in negative behaviour and the damaging consequences that can arise from the lack of opportunities and facilities in particular neighbourhoods.

Prior, 2007, pp. 15, 17–18

Comment

Although here the policy goal was once again crime prevention, in this case, the focus was more directly on initiatives concerned with the welfare of children and families (see **McCarthy, 2008**, for a wider discussion of the tensions within family policy). Support, rather than enforcement, was the key underlying principle. In this context, although there is no explicit reference to 'community', the emphasis on linkages at 'neighbourhood' level implies a more positive set of possibilities through an increased focus on opportunities rather than constraints.

Figure 2.4
Tony Blair, Prime Minister at the time, meets young people in the inner city

Activity 2.4

In the next case, the research focused on the effects of a community engagement strategy aimed at empowering local residents by giving them opportunities to become directly involved in the governance of their area, with the expectation that this would also work to reduce levels of crime and antisocial behaviour.

When reading Extract 2.3, you should consider two main issues:

■ the extent to which the problems identified can be resolved at the level of community

■ the extent to which even well-intentioned initiatives may have a negative rather than a positive impact.

Extract 2.3

Whilst our research indicated some specific successes in this strategy of community engagement, the overall picture was one of considerable difficulty being encountered in generating lasting and effective citizen participation; where it was occurring it tended to involve very small numbers of people, and often people who had a long history of such activity. It was clearly difficult to find new participants in the various initiatives and particularly to recruit younger participants. Perhaps the starkest example of such difficulty was provided by the Neighbourhood Safety Project: this was concerned with an estate where the residents identified high levels of crime and anti-social behaviour as a major problem, yet very few residents appeared willing to become engaged with the project.

One explanation for the difficulties encountered by the community engagement strategy seemed to us, as researchers, to be that the substantial problems faced by many residents in their everyday lives – problems of poverty, unemployment, poor housing, poor health, lack of local resources and facilities, and so on, as well as problems of crime and ASB [antisocial behaviour] – meant that there was little confidence that their participation in the process of governance would lead to any positive change. This pessimism was tied into a profound lack of trust in either the willingness or capacity of the public agencies to take action that might lead to sustained improvement in the socio-economic conditions of the area. The consequence was a widespread lack of both the energy required to engage in participation and the belief that it would actually make any difference.

...

There was, however, another major factor that seemed to us to act as an inhibitor to the effective implementation of the community engagement strategy. This was that the formal agencies were also pursuing a strategy of enforcement in their attempt to address problems of ASB, and the two strategies were sometimes in conflict with each other. Thus the local authority and, especially, the police were keen to demonstrate that they were taking seriously the problem of ASB (which had been identified by the public as a priority concern) and to do so by deploying, and being seen to deploy, the range of powers available under the ASB legislation. Thus there was a strong commitment to respond to specific instances of ASB through the use of various enforcement technologies – ASBOs, the closure of crack houses, the creation of dispersal zones – and to publicise these measures whenever possible. This action had contradictory impacts on the local communities. Whilst it was clear that many residents welcomed a hard line being taken to deal with behaviour they found intolerable, it was also apparent that the use of such technologies generated tensions. Thus, residents in one area felt that they were being stigmatized and over-regulated by excessive enforcement activities, at the same time as expressing doubts about how effective such action actually was; while in another, similar, area residents complained that the problems of ASB that they faced were not being addressed with the same level of seriousness. Such issues contributed to the general sense of a lack of confidence by residents in the local agencies, which helped undermine the attempts at community engagement.

Prior, 2007, pp. 22, 23

Comment

This research suggests that community-based policies often cannot in themselves resolve the problems on which they are targeted. The second paragraph in Extract 2.3 lists a series of significant problems faced by residents that originate in wider social structures and patterns of inequality. The research also suggests that the tensions between pursuing an enforcement (disciplinary or punitive) strategy and an enabling or supportive one make it difficult to achieve the broader policy ambitions of community development and civil renewal. Achieving an appropriate balance is not straightforward (see also **Cochrane and Talbot, 2008a**).

Despite all apparently being directed towards the same desired outcome, the three studies reported in the activities above show some of the different ways in which community is understood. And they also confirm the tensions associated with public policy attempts to engage with the various communities involved. They highlight not only the complex ways in which social welfare and crime control policies are entangled in the practice of community-based policy, and the ways in which apparently welfare-oriented initiatives become associated with more punitive forms of intervention, but also the ways in which initiatives apparently driven by a punitive agenda may be associated with approaches providing social support.

Extract 2.1 focuses on the need to change behaviour over the longer term, but also confirms that a contractual approach to antisocial behaviour may be undermined by the wider problems faced by families and communities. The extract suggests that the families involved are dysfunctional, which means that not only are their parenting skills underdeveloped, but the broader (community) context makes it unlikely that any particular family will be able to escape. Here the complex interaction of children at risk and being identified as potentially dangerous seems to generate an inescapable downward spiral (see also **McCarthy, 2008**).

Extract 2.2 is more directly oriented towards issues of risk and riskiness. The emphasis is on preventing the 'social exclusion' of children by seeking to meet wider social needs and to offer constructive opportunities. In other words, this is an approach that starts from the problems faced by children and looks for ways of overcoming them – but it relies on their readiness to take the opportunities available.

Extract 2.3 again takes a different approach to community, aiming to encourage the involvement and engagement of community members. However, here the research indicates that, in practice, too few have been ready to get involved. The explanation for that failure lies in the substantial problems faced by residents, which means that there is a lack of trust in the agencies looking for cooperation. Strategies of enforcement, leading to punitive intervention, are also seen to get in the way of trust and its development, and there are doubts among community members about both the effectiveness of such interventions (because disorder continues to be an issue for some) and their targeting (because some feel themselves to be unfairly targeted). The question of 'who gets involved' – and the possible consequences of their involvement – is the focus of Section 4.

4 Community activism and community policy

As we have shown, the notion of community is an ambivalent and ambiguous, but a politically (or 'rhetorically') very useful, one, particularly for those seeking to construct a politics of collective and individual responsibility. A fundamental principle that underlies the rise of community policy is the belief that communities can – in some way – act for themselves. Communities are also often seen as spaces within which those who need to be reintegrated into society can be assisted in doing so, almost by a process of social osmosis. The underpinning assumptions of 'care in the community', for example, discussed in Section 2, suggest that it is better for people to remain in the 'community' where they engage in a series of ordinary social interactions, rather than being removed to a protected but isolated institutional setting. The implication is also that those being cared for will be watched over informally without being subject to the more formal, and not always so caring, attention of people with only a professional responsibility for their oversight. Similarly, community sentencing implies that requiring criminals to engage in activities that draw them closer to community networks will integrate them more into the positive aspects of community life and so make them less likely to engage in antisocial or criminal behaviour. These issues are considered in different ways in this section. The notion of community has been used to underpin approaches to the management of diverse populations, as well as a means to target forms of welfare intervention more effectively and to mobilise members of the community to take on new social responsibilities.

Figure 2.5
Meeting of a
partnership board

There is a long history in the UK and the USA of area-based or neighbourhood-based 'community' intervention. And in recent years, the notion of community has been increasingly central to strategies aimed at challenging poverty, particularly when focused on the regeneration or renewal of particular neighbourhoods. In large part, this draws on the assumption that 'Communities themselves ought to be the best advocates of their own interests' (Social Exclusion Unit, 2000, para. 2.17). But the 'erosion of social capital' – that is, 'the contact, trust and solidarity that enables residents to help, rather than fear, each other' – has also been identified as one of the main weaknesses facing deprived communities (Social Exclusion Unit, 2000, para. 8). Reversing this trend, therefore, is seen as a precondition for successful community development.

The key debates about 'social capital' were introduced in Chapter 1. Social capital, according to Robert Putnam, 'refers to features of social organisation such as networks, norms and trust that facilitate co-ordination and co-operation for mutual benefit. Social capital enhances the benefits of investment in physical and human capital' (Putnam, 1993, p. 35). In policy terms, this has increasingly been translated into the notion of capacity building – the building of community capacity. As one community activist argues:

> civil renewal, particularly in the neighbourhoods where people live, will not take place either as a result of well meaning volunteers from elsewhere or the state from above, but from the direct involvement of the people who live there. They must manage, own and staff the process of renewal and they must have access to the vast budgets of the disastrous one-size-fits-all services of which everyone complains and which produce dependent servitude. ...

> It entails building the capacity of the dispossessed to help themselves, to change the circumstances in which they live from ones which blight their lives to ones which transform and liberate them.
> (Atkinson, 2004, p. 38)

Similar arguments have been taken up in the language of official policy where the claim has been made that 'Self-help is an end in itself, as well as a means to an end. It is at the core of the empowerment of communities ... about involvement and consultation but also about moving towards self-sufficiency ... about communities shaping their own destiny – doing, not being done to' (Home Office, 1999, para. 1.3).

The process, however, is not straightforward. Drawing on notions of community as a means of changing the behaviour of particular populations has also generated challenges from those, within the 'communities', whose behaviour is to be changed. While an emphasis on community may be intended to encourage a higher degree of self-discipline and self-policing among those populations, new tensions may also be generated (some of the implications of this are discussed by Sharon Pinkney and Esther Saraga in Chapter 5 of this book). Community work has a long colonial prehistory, when it was associated with the drive to generate identifiable 'communities' with leaders with whom it was possible for the colonial rulers to work (see, for example, Mayo, 1975). This continues to be reflected in attempts to draw on, involve and potentially even create community activists in the delivery (and sometimes the development) of policy. John Clarke explicitly places the politics and policy practices of 'community' in their postcolonial context, highlighting the ways in which they engage with notions of 'multiculturalism', so that communities of difference become identified with particular neighbourhoods and suitable sites for intervention, for targeted management and the building of normality (Clarke, 2002; see also Chapter 3 in this volume).

The advice given in the 1997 edition of *Involving Communities* (DETR, 1997) could have been lifted from guidance given in the colonial era. It emphasises the need to consult each identifiable ethnic group and to 'Show you have the support of accepted leaders but are not in their pocket' (quoted in Chanan, 2003, p. 34). Manawar Jahn-Khan forcefully questions traditional approaches to community development, as used in working with minority ethnic communities in British cities, because of the way in which government agencies seek to work through recognised 'leaders'. He suggests not only that these approaches are legacies of the old colonial approaches, but also that they help to define the community itself as 'difficult' – only to be managed through those leaders (Jahn-Khan, 2003, p. 41).

Activity 2.5

Extract 2.4 is taken from a case study of 'Shoreditch Our Way' (SHOW), a community-based partnership in East London, which was part of a wider national community-based initiative (Perrons and Skyers, 2003). It highlights some of the key issues arising from community involvement in such projects. It identifies three different sets of people: local authority officers, community representatives and tenant representatives. All were members of the Board – the governing body of this partnership-based initiative.

As you read Extract 2.4:

■ try to identify the tensions between these three sets of people

■ suggest factors that may have led to those tensions.

Extract 2.4

What does recognition and empowerment mean in practice?

Community empowerment implies that people will have the necessary information, as well as power and influence to exercise some control over the future of their area. There were, however, widely diverging views [between local authority offices, RENAISI, a not-for-profit development company involved in regeneration, and the SHOW Board] over the extent of the community's control. For example, one local authority officer remarked on the perceived independence of the SHOW partnership:

> I think, you know, some of our partnerships are going down avenues the Council doesn't agree with [...] and we're watching with interest

[...] The Council is very un-influential in that partnership and people down there are doing some good things and making some mistakes and if they worked better with us, they wouldn't be making those mistakes, but at least they own those mistakes (ID 4 Local Authority Officer).

In practical terms, however, some members of the community felt that the major funding agencies generally determined the degree of control and influence local people could exercise, and over which decisions. One SHOW Board member put it this way:

all the ideas that we had and wanted to put in place, because they didn't meet some formal government criteria, they disappeared. They didn't match the same speed at which we were working. We would put special projects together and they would disappear into the never never (ID 1 Resident and SHOW Board Member).

This comment also reflects how local participation takes place within centrally prescribed parameters and procedures. Other participants questioned whether local control was actually genuine or desirable, and saw it as a means of passing responsibility to the community for problems officials had been grappling with but had failed to resolve. One local tenant representative made the following observation:

I'm just speaking for myself here, but I think Tony Blair [UK Prime Minister at the time] has given people like us too much responsibility too soon. We're not experienced people. I mean, I can't understand a lot of things the Consultants say, I think he's plunged us in at the deep end that's what I think (ID 2 Tenant Representative and SHOW Board Member).

However, other local people argued that real empowerment was about the community having the freedom to make mistakes particularly as local government officials had been making mistakes for years and had left the community to suffer the consequences. Other respondents were more cautious and suggested that a longer time horizon was needed to get the community discussing ideas about what it would like to see, arguing that discussions about priorities should take place before any significant spending was undertaken.

Perrons and Skyers, 2003, p. 279

Comment

The tensions between some of the different groups involved come out in the words of the local authority and community representatives. For the local authority representative, there is a real fear that the project and the Board (with its community representatives) may take on a life of its own and bypass the council; for the community representative, the process seems designed to remove community priorities from the agenda through negotiation; while for the tenant representative, the problem is identified as a lack of training when confronted by experts and consultants. There is a tension between the priorities identified by community representatives (for short-term improvement) and those identified by consultants and government representatives (for longer-term strategic development).

Diane Perrons and Sophia Skyers (2003, p. 266) go on to argue that community participation works only if it gives access to 'decisions over allocation of material resources', which most community initiatives do not. However, it is also necessary to recognise the sharp tensions that may exist within places that are understood as communities – or more modestly as 'neighbourhoods'. The authors point to the existence of real, material differences within 'communities', which mean that it is not possible to generate a simple and unified 'vision' capable of bringing them together. So, for example, they note that one tenant representative on the Board was against the demolition of some blocks of flats to provide houses for younger people, while another favoured the demolition of some to make it easier to do up those that remained. Communities are not inert and homogeneous spaces just waiting to be engaged in the policy process, but are themselves (as Hoggett, 1997, notes) highly 'contested'.

The management of 'communities', whether by themselves or through state professionals, is complex and uncertain. There is a continuing tension between the strategic priorities of the professionals to implement policies and the attempt to involve residents or community members, whose priorities may be rather different.

The involvement of community and tenant representatives on the governing bodies of community initiatives creates new forms of expertise, because such representatives work with professionals and come, perhaps, to share some of their knowledge, skills and orientations. This dramatic spread of 'professionalism', both into community and voluntary organisations and into those areas of the state that have the responsibility of managing them, creates new sets of relationships and defines new sets of 'obligation'. As social policy analysts Wendy Larner and David Craig note in their review of community activism and local partnerships in New Zealand, community organisations themselves become a source of 'de-centralised professional and technical' expertise (Larner and Craig, 2005, p. 409). One possible consequence of this might be that local activists become incorporated into wider state agendas through professionalisation. The danger of this is powerfully summed up in strong language in the response of one woman to a newly professionalised community activist (about to move out of the local area): 'You've fucked up the estate and now you're carrying a briefcase' (McCulloch, 1997, p. 51).

However, Larner and Craig explore more positively the ways in which the rise of state-sponsored local partnerships has generated the need for what they call 'strategic brokers'; that is, people with 'an ability to network and promote change' (Larner and Craig, 2005, p. 404). They suggest that such people are frequently drawn from the ranks of community activists (and are often women), providing 'new roles for those who were oppositional voices' (Larner and Craig, 2005, p. 418). It is they who have the key soft skills as 'advocates both for their organisations and more relational forms of practice' with both 'knowledge *of* communities' but also, as they develop their professionalism, 'knowledge *about* communities' (Larner and Craig, 2005, pp. 415, 418).

Larner and Craig are not alone in highlighting the gendered basis of much community engagement. Drawing on the US experience, social theorist Melissa Gilbert suggests that an approach drawing on 'feminist conceptualizations of multiple power relations, agency, daily life, politics, community and place can enhance our understanding of the daily lives of poor women in cities as well as their contribution to the production of urban space and politics' (Gilbert, 1999, p. 107). In her research in Colorado and Washington state in the USA, geographer Lynn Staeheli (2003) charts a range of strategies developed by women working in community-based social care organisations 'as a basis for building an inclusive society in which social justice can be achieved through an ethic of care' (Staeheli, 2003, p. 816). In other words, they are engaged in an active process seeking to deliver change and not simply manage survival in a relatively hostile environment. While the relationship between the growing professional role and the community role is not an easy one (Larner and Craig, 2005, describe it as 'fraught'), it cannot be dismissed simply as a process of incorporation.

Activity 2.6

In this section, we have presented you with optimistic and pessimistic views about the potential of community engagement. The pessimistic view has highlighted the unforeseen consequences; for example, the possibility of the incorporation or professionalisation of community activists, or the ways in which communities that are drawn into engagement with various initiatives may later be disappointed as promises are not delivered or funding is not sustained. The optimistic view tends towards seeing community engagement as a form of empowerment of those in poverty and marginalised from mainstream social and political life. Here we suggest that you look back at Extracts 2.1 to 2.3 from Prior (2007) in Section 3. Do you think these gave an optimistic or a pessimistic view? And, more importantly, what do you think the factors might be that create the kinds of engagement that mobilise social change within – and perhaps beyond – a particular place-bound community?

Comment

There is no straightforward answer to these questions. The evidence can be read in different ways. However, we think that it is neither helpful simply to dismiss communities (or neighbourhoods) as bases for active engagement with the potential to reshape the lives of those who live in them, nor simply to celebrate their potential as sources of dynamism. The challenge is, rather, as Marilyn Taylor says:

> to find creative ways of equipping those who are politically, socially and economically excluded to find and exploit the cracks and tensions within the system and the windows of opportunity they create. The role for those who want to support community change, in this analysis, is to make power visible, identify the opportunities for change, and to ensure that communities are ready and have the skills to exploit them. This means working with communities over the long term, linking people up, creating the spaces and energies for co-operative enquiry and exploration, sharing and understanding experience. It means spreading involvement, and keeping things going through the thin times, so that organisational intelligence ... and networks are there when they are needed. It means acting as a 'social relay' to link up the people across different systems who can mobilise to exploit opportunities for change. It means finding the allies whose external resources provide communities with resources they cannot command on their own ... and pushing at the edges of what is possible.
>
> (Taylor, 2003, p. 224)

Much (although not all) of the research we have referred to in this chapter was undertaken in the UK, specifically England and Wales. But notions of community have a much wider policy resonance. Community may speak to the local, the personal, and the daily processes of social interaction, but it has also, for example, been the focus of policy intended as a response to seemingly intractable global problems of poverty; for instance, the policy initiatives driven through by agencies such as the World Bank and UN-HABITAT (see also **Cochrane and Walters, 2008**; Chapter 6 of this volume). Increased stress is placed on the potential of communities, particularly those of the urban 'slums' and rural settlements, to generate new forms of entrepreneurialism and dynamic innovation through informal networks, rather than the formal institutions of the state (or, indeed, the market). The broad model is one that moves away from the provision of 'handouts', or even provision of services to poor people, to one that seeks to draw the poor into the process of growth. But behind the rhetoric of empowerment lies the shadow of compulsion. Such strategies are directed towards nation states viewed as in need of 'development', and where development is supported by agencies such as the World Bank, it tends to come with strings attached (Whitford and Mathur, 2006). This takes us back to the ambiguities around the use of community in public policy: the difficult relationship between 'activism' and 'incorporation' and between 'empowerment' and 'compulsion', and the entanglement between welfare-oriented approaches to social inclusion and crime control strategies.

5   Review

This chapter has opened up a range of ways in which 'community' is utilised in the development and implementation of policy. To help you review these, we want to return to some of the ideas you met in Chapter 1. There you were introduced to four ways in which community has been thought of:

■ community as a spatial concept

■ communities as non-spatial sites of identity and culture

■ communities as boundaries and sites of conflict

■ communities as sites of citizenship and governance.

Examples of all these ways of thinking about community can be found throughout this chapter. Many of the extracts from advertisements in Section 2 reflect an understanding of community as a spatial concept – it is the place in which the successful applicants will be doing their jobs, and the boundaries of their engagement are spatially defined. Policies designed to help tackle inequality and disadvantage appear to be linked to place-based policies of community development, which are often informed by a stronger spatial sense of identity and culture. However, we also saw references to ideas such as the 'multicultural' community, suggesting non-spatial communities based on presumed similarities of identity and culture; as well as examples of communities as (potential) sites of conflict.

Similarly, all the cases discussed in Section 3 focused on area-based initiatives, in which, implicitly as well as explicitly, community was understood as place based. In some of the examples, forms of community development (particularly when associated with family policy) were seen as offering positive opportunities, while in others the nature of neighbourhood social relations was identified as the problem – generating conflict and antisocial behaviour. In at least one of the cases, the underlying assumption of policy development seemed to be that community governance (see Chapters 1 and 4) would help generate civic responsibility even if the potential for such development was undermined by more disciplinary (and even punitive) approaches to the management of social behaviour.

Section 4 considered further some of the tensions and contradictions in the relationship between community activism and community governance. By implication, at least, much of the discussion draws on a place-based notion of community, but it also highlights some of the difficulties of defining communities in this way – pointing to the divisions within communities as well as between them. The case study of Shoreditch showed that communities are important policy sites through which citizenship is defined, both because of the way in which their members make their claims to be heard, and because of the way in which it is hoped they will learn to manage their own lives.

In other words, what is interesting in the policy process is the way in which the various categories come together in different ways. In this context, the notion of community also illuminates the entanglements between social welfare and crime control. Here, the issue is not so much (or at least not only) the tension or contradiction between enforcement and support, but rather, the way in which the two are uneasily intertwined in practice. Community-based policies offer both the prospect of encouraging community members to learn to behave responsibly (in the terms of those who have developed the policies) and the opportunity to find ways of developing claims to resources and potentially finding ways of managing their own lives in unexpected ways. As Clarke puts it: 'Community remains a peculiar place to govern, because people consistently refuse to "know their place"' (Clarke, 2002, p. 13).

To help ground these debates, in this chapter we have focused on a range of different kinds of evidence. The extracts in Section 2 point to the ways in which even job advertisements, produced for quite a different set of purposes, can provide a rich source of data about how the language of community has informed a reordering of the relationship between policymaking and citizenship. We looked carefully at the language of the advertisements to suggest ways in which 'community' was understood in relationship to the words surrounding it in a short piece of text. Ideas such as community can have very different political associations: they may be part of the vocabulary of both the radical left and social movements, opposing oppressive forms of state power and fighting for social justice (see **Newman and Yeates, 2008**), and of the conservative right (seeking stronger moral bonds as the source of social order). 'Community' is associated with activists, seeking change 'from below', and with new forms of the state or 'governance', attempting to steer policy 'from above'.

The evidence gathered in the pieces of research in Sections 3 and 4 is based on talking to those who are actually delivering policy, and to those who experience its implementation. It involves listening to their accounts and considering what they say. The value of this form of research – often called qualitative research – is that it allows for in-depth discussion and produces detailed reflection on particular initiatives. It makes it possible to explore how the people involved interpret the process of policymaking and its effects, and to follow up particular concerns. It is sometimes argued, however, that this kind of research may be misleading because it gives particular people (i.e. those interviewed) a voice that others do not have. That is one of the reasons why the researchers draw on a range of different sources. It is also sometimes suggested that one of the problems with research of this kind is that it finds it difficult to reflect on outcomes – in other words, it may bring together several views of what is happening without ever considering what has or has not been achieved in practice. However, it is precisely the attempt to understand outcomes that has driven the research discussed in this chapter.

Further reading

The role of community in the development of policy is very helpfully discussed by Marilyn Taylor in her book *Public Policy in the Community* (2003, Palgrave Macmillan). While well aware of some of the tensions and contradictions in community-based policy, she also points to some of the ways in which a focus on community can generate positive change. For a book which celebrates the potential of community as a means of resolving social problems, delivering social welfare and challenging antisocial behaviour and criminality, it would be worth looking at Dick Atkinson's *Civil Renewal: Mending the Hole in the Social Ozone Layer* (2004, Brewin Books). Community has been and is likely to continue to be at the centre of a series of government publications – it will be worth keeping an eye out for these as they are produced. The Commission on Integration and Cohesion's report on *Our Shared Future* (2007) is a particularly interesting attempt to deal with the tensions between the notion of community as a source of social cohesion and as a source of division.

References

Atkinson, D. (2004) *Civil Renewal: Mending the Hole in the Social Ozone Layer*, Studley, Brewin Books.

Chanan, G. (2003) *Searching for Solid Foundations: Community Involvement and Urban Policy*, London, Office of the Deputy Prime Minister.

Clarke, J. (2002) 'Reinventing community? Governing in contested spaces', paper presented at *Spacing Social Work – On the Territorialization of the Social* conference, Bielefeld, 14–16 November.

Clarke, J. (2008) 'Looking for social justice: welfare states and beyond' in Newman and Yeates (eds) (2008).

Cochrane, A. and Talbot, D. (2008a) 'The search for security' in Cochrane and Talbot (eds) (2008b).

Cochrane, A. and Talbot, D. (eds) (2008b) *Security: Welfare, Crime and Society*, Maidenhead, Open University Press/Milton Keynes, The Open University.

Cochrane, A. and Walters, R. (2008) 'The globalisation of social justice' in Newman and Yeates (eds) (2008).

Commission on Integration and Cohesion (2007) *Final Report: Our Shared Future*, London, Commission on Integration and Cohesion.

Department of the Environment, Transport and the Regions (DETR) (1997) *Involving Communities*, London, Department of the Environment, Transport and the Regions.

Edwards, A., Barnes, M., Plewis, I. and Morris, K. et al. (2006) *Working to Prevent the Social Exclusion of Children and Young People: Final Lessons from the National Evaluation of the Children's Fund*, Research Report RR 734, London, Department for Education and Skills.

Fergusson, R. and Muncie, J. (2008) 'Criminalising conduct' in Cochrane and Talbot (eds) (2008b).

Gilbert, M. (1999) 'Place, politics, and the production of urban space: a feminist critique of the growth machine thesis' in Jonas, A. and Wilson, D. (eds) *The Urban Growth Machine: Critical Perspectives Two Decades Later*, Albany, NY, State University of New York Press.

Hoggett, P. (ed.) (1997) *Contested Communities: Experiences, Struggles, Policies*, Bristol, The Policy Press.

Home Office (1999) *Report of the Policy Action Team on Community Self-Help*, PAT Report No. 9, London, Active Community Unit, Home Office.

Jahn-Khan, M. (2003) 'The right to riot?', *Community Development Journal*, vol. 38, no. 1, pp. 32–42.

Jewkes, Y. (2008) 'Insecurity, fear and social retreat' in Cochrane and Talbot (eds) (2008b).

Johnstone, C. (2004) 'Crime, disorder and the urban renaissance' in Johnstone and Whitehead (eds) (2004).

Johnstone, C. and Whitehead, M. (eds) (2004) *New Horizons in British Urban Policy: Perspectives on New Labour's Urban Renaissance*, Aldershot, Ashgate.

Larner, W. and Craig, D. (2005) 'After neo-liberalism? Community activism in social partnerships in Aotearoa, New Zealand', *Antipode*, vol. 37, no. 3, pp. 402–24.

McCarthy, J.R. (2008) 'Security, insecurity and family lives' in Cochrane and Talbot (eds) (2008b).

McCulloch, A. (1997) 'You've fucked up the estate and now you're carrying a briefcase!' in Hoggett, P. (ed.) *Contested Communities: Experiences, Struggles, Policies*, Bristol, The Policy Press.

Mason, P. and Prior, D. (2006) *The Children's Fund and the Reduction of Crime and Anti-social Behaviour*, Birmingham, University of Birmingham.

Mayo, M. (1975) 'The history and early development of CDP' in Lees, R. and Brake, M. (eds) *Action Research in Community Development*, London, Routledge and Kegan Paul.

Mooney, G. (2008) '"Problem" populations, "problem" places' in Newman and Yeates (eds) (2008).

Myhill, A. (2006) *Community Engagement in Policing: Lessons from the Literature*, London, Home Office; also available online at http://www.crimereduction.homeoffice.gov.uk/policing18.htm (Accessed 4 April 2008).

Newman, J. and Yeates, N. (eds) (2008) *Social Justice: Welfare, Crime and Society*, Maidenhead, Open University Press/Milton Keynes, The Open University.

Perrons, D. and Skyers, S. (2003) 'Empowerment through participation? Conceptual explorations and a case study', *International Journal of Urban and Regional Research*, vol. 27, no. 2, pp. 265–85.

Prior, D. (2006) *Evaluation of the Choices Project*, Birmingham, University of Birmingham.

Prior, D. (2007) *Continuities and Discontinuities in Governing Anti-Social Behaviour*, Birmingham, Institute of Applied Social Studies, University of Birmingham.

Prior, D., Farrow, K., Spalek, B. and Barnes, M. (2006) 'Anti-social behaviour and civil renewal' in Brennan, T., John, P. and Stoker, G. (eds) *Re-energising Citizenship: Strategies for Civil Renewal*, London, Palgrave.

Putnam, R. (1993) *Making Democracy Work: Civic Traditions in Modern Italy*, Princeton, NJ, Princeton University Press.

Social Exclusion Unit (2000) *National Strategy for Neighbourhood Renewal: A Framework for Consultation*, London, Cabinet Office.

Staeheli, L. (2003) 'Women and the work of community', *Environment and Planning A*, 35, part 5, pp. 815–31.

Taylor, M. (2003) *Public Policy in the Community*, Basingstoke, Palgrave Macmillan.

Whitehead, M. (2004) 'The urban neighbourhood and the moral geographies of British urban policy' in Johnstone and Whitehead (eds) (2004).

Whitford, P. and Mathur, K. (2006) *The Effectiveness of World Bank Support for Community-based and -driven Development*, Washington, DC, The World Bank.

Chapter 3
Community, social change and social order

John Clarke

Contents

1   Introduction

This chapter takes up some of the core issues about community established in Chapters 1 and 2. It connects aspects of the study of community in the social sciences to questions about the current enthusiasm for community in both popular and policy thinking. Central to the chapter is the question: *what makes community a recurrent aspiration: something that people seek and try to bring into being?* Section 2 offers some answers to this question, examining different *desires for community*, while Section 3 explores one particular way of trying to create and *secure community* – the phenomenon of 'gated communities'. Section 4 returns to questions about the *meanings of community*, and explores three different sources of contemporary ideas about community: images of the rural community; images of the industrial or working-class community; and images of the colonial community. Section 5 explores what is at stake when different images of community collide, raising questions about the relationships between people and places, and about different sorts of *belonging*.

Underlying the chapter is a concern with how popular, policy and academic ideas about community are caught up with issues of *social change* and *social order*, and the final section uses these as a way of reviewing the chapter. You have already seen in the previous two chapters how community can refer to a sense of loss or nostalgia (the 'golden age' of community) and to aspirations for the future (communities can be built, enabled, developed, supported). Similarly, community can evoke images of social order (integration, stability and security) and images of more *dis*ordered social arrangements (from dysfunctional communities to processes of exclusion and marginalisation).

The aims of this chapter are therefore to:

■ examine the reasons as to why the idea of community is so desirable

■ consider, in particular, strategies to secure or 'make' community

■ reflect on how the different meanings of community relate to questions and ideas of social change and social order.

2   Desiring community?

In the extracts from job advertisements given in Figure 2.1 in Chapter 2, community was associated with a variety of positive words. Here are some of the ones that took my eye:

■ 'fresh vision'

■ 'brighter service for everyone in our community'

- 'make a difference' (three times)

- 'A new and vibrant service [in a] ... vibrant and multicultural community'

- 'a constant, reassuring presence'

- 'all our communities to thrive'

- 'involvement in key decision-making'

- 'local leaders'.

All of these, as Allan Cochrane and Janet Newman have argued, point to the power and appeal of community as a term in political and policy discourses. But, as Chapter 1 highlights, the word clearly has appeal beyond the academic, political and policy worlds – it also circulates freely in everyday life. It is a popular 'keyword' (Williams, 1976). In this section, I want to spend a little time thinking about why many people might be enthusiastic about living in, or being a member of, a community.

Activity 3.1

Stop for a moment and make a note of why you think people might find the idea of 'being a member of a community' attractive.

Comment

I can think of many reasons for wanting to be a member of a community. It evokes ideas of identification, belonging, or attachment, for example. It carries a sense of sharing experiences or orientations with others. Here though, I want to suggest that there may be four popular desires that can be expressed through the aspiration or ideal of 'community'. These are the desires for:

- restoration

- security

- sociality

- solidarity.

In the rest of this section, I will look at each of these ideas in a little more detail.

The desire for *restoration* involves the belief that a real or imagined past order of social relationships might be revived: a way of life that felt in some ways more orderly, predictable, or comfortable. Community is often used to describe a sense of loss – a nostalgia for a better way of life. It implies a time when *social relationships* were more transparent, more warm, more trustworthy or more egalitarian than in the present. Similarly, *social conduct* was better: people behaved in ways that were more respectful, more civil and more interdependent than in the present. Finally, this past time was also marked by a stronger sense of *social order*: patterns of behaviour were more disciplined, more authoritative and more predictable than in the present.

Figure 3.1

Castle Combe, Wiltshire: village life as the ideal community?

This idea of community as restoration links notions of communal or shared experiences and interrelationships with models of the social authority needed to hold society – and community – together. Such images of community point to complex mixtures of intimacy and authority where trust is the effect of mutual knowledge (as against a society of strangers) and where order is the consequence of a system of positions, power and deference. In such conceptions of community, people 'know their place'. If society is experienced as becoming more unpredictable or uncertain, nostalgia for ordered relationships might be seen as a likely form of desire. Let me emphasise that this nostalgia/ restoration mixture does not necessarily mean that earlier periods of social life were in fact more orderly, disciplined or community based. As cultural theorist Raymond Williams (1985, p. 35) argued, each period of British history has identified a lost golden age in which traditional society, ways of life and values or virtues existed – and have been eroded by social change. More recently, Paul Watt suggests that these mythical rural golden ages are paralleled by 'narratives of urban decline' in which 'the intimate social relations of yesteryear ("the community") were said to be no more' (Watt, 2006, p. 782; see also the example of Harry Bernstein in Chapter 1). What matters is that people desire community *through a belief* that society used to be that way – and that, by reconstructing community, some (real or imagined) old certainties might be restored. What we see here is the intimate and difficult connection between ideas of *social order* and processes of *social change*.

Security is a related desire, linked by a sense of the growing unpredictability and uncertainty of social life. For example, sociologist Richard Sennett (2006, pp. 23–6, 48–54) has discussed the fragmentation and dislocation of time in the 'culture of the new capitalism' affecting everything from ideas of the 'working day' to notions of social progress and personal development (e.g. in conceptions of 'having a career'). He suggests that these changes have also dislocated the sense of how individual security and collective security were connected in the post-Second World War societies of 'welfare capitalism' (Esping-Andersen, 1990). In such societies, individual life courses were locked into employment systems and state welfare systems for the majority of the population. Security meant security of employment, and public support for housing, family formation and collective insurance (sometimes called 'social security') against the risks of illness, unemployment and ageing. In contrast, contemporary policies emphasise the importance of people not relying on the state, but being 'active citizens' who take 'responsibility' for their own lives and well-being (Clarke, 2005). Such changes disrupt existing systems and patterns of life associated with them, creating anxiety about risk, vulnerability and *dis*order (there are important links here to other debates about security in contemporary welfare and crime control policy: see **Cochrane and Talbot, 2008**; Hughes, 2007).

I use the word *sociality* to identify a desire for 'transparent' human interactions, in which people engage with each other as equals. Such interactions can occur only if people are free of what might be called 'antisocial' pressures. These might be force or coercion (involving inequalities of power, and violence), or the impact of cynical or calculative frameworks (in which people make decisions based on their own cost or advantage). Desires for sociality are not necessarily nostalgic or restorationist: they do not always imply a past in which such transparent interactions took place. Rather, they may speak to an aspiration – community to come – in which people behave better towards one another in their encounters, whether as friends, neighbours or strangers. Ironically, people may look to 'traditional' societies as models of such sociality, seeing them as less mediated, less artificial and less calculative than 'modern life' (you might remember the comments about rural communities from the research study that featured in Chapter 1). Both the market and the state appear as institutions that have 'antisocial' effects – interrupting or distorting proper human interaction (Studdert, 2005). Markets and states induce bad or inauthentic forms of behaviour instead of humane interactions because they put calculating frameworks – of cost, power or advantage – in between people. Phrases like 'money talks' or 'it's just politics' express popular disdain for such ways of thinking and behaving.

Finally, *solidarity* denotes desires for collective identification and the possibilities of collective action. Community is one of the forms in which we can envisage collectivity – articulating or expressing common concerns, values or interests (see also Chapter 5 in this volume). Solidarity is about *shared* experiences, positions or aspirations. More than this, however, it is also about the transcendence or suspension of difference: the construction of a common purpose despite differences. Communities can mobilise to change things (e.g. create an adequate water supply), to demand things (e.g. social justice) or to protect things (e.g. defend a local hospital against threatened closure). Such mobilisation requires the construction of a collective identification based on some principle (a shared place, position, experience or orientation) in ways that overcome differences or potential divisions. Community as an expression of solidarity works by being able to imagine *commonality across difference*. That is to say, community as solidarity involves foregrounding what 'we' have in common, and downplaying differences: 'people like us' have to be constructed. Solidarity speaks of recurrent desires to mobilise and be mobilised and to engage in the promise that the world (or this part of it) might be different: issues to which you will return in Chapter 5.

These four desires might be summarised as in Table 3.1 opposite. The list given there is certainly not exhaustive, but it might be enough to suggest why community has popular as well as political significance (see also Creed, 2006). Few other terms have the capacity to evoke and contain such powerful desires – and their associated images of how life might be lived. Community speaks to us powerfully: about images of order, security, shared values and future possibilities. It is a word that promises comfort, strength, settlement and even transformation.

Table 3.1 Desiring community

Desire	Basis	Image of community
Restoration	Nostalgia; sense of loss; *dis*order; lack of authority	Social order; intimacy combined with authority; people 'know their place'
Security	Anxiety; insecurity; uncertainty; disorder; crime, danger, especially 'stranger danger'	Social order; predictability; authority; 'people like us'
Sociality	Alienated or mistrustful social relationships, corrupted by instrumental calculation (political, economic or personal)	Transparent, humane social relationships; trust and openness; mutuality
Solidarity	Common experiences of exclusion, oppression, injustice or being wronged	People in motion; collective mobilisations to construct 'people like us' who act, make demands or protest

3 Securing community?

One of the most dramatic ways in which people have tried to find a sense of community is through the construction of 'gated communities': a space of enclosure, surrounded by physical barriers (such as walls, fences) to which access is controlled through an entry system. Some use private security staff to control access, and sometimes to patrol internally. Although the USA has the largest proportion of such residential developments, the practice of building gated communities has spread globally as some people look to create both a sense of community and a sense of security in what are perceived as dangerous, risky or threatening urban spaces (see **Jewkes, 2008**).

In this section, I will be drawing on a study by a US researcher, Setha Low, who visited gated communities and talked to people who lived within them about their search for community and security. I am focusing on gated communities here because they represent a particularly intense version of what creating or constructing community might involve. As such, they might also be a focus for intensely felt *desires* for community. This explains why this section draws extensively on Setha Low's study: her interest is precisely in the mix of feelings and experiences involved in people's desires for community and the choice of a gated community as a way of trying to make those desires come true. Although much has been written about gated communities, Low's

Figure 3.2
Securing community?
A US gated community

study stands out because of this attention to the experiential, emotional and affective dimensions of people's relationships to such developments. Let us begin with a couple of extracts from her interviews.

Activity 3.2

Read Extract 3.1 below. As you do so, make a note of what you think are the key themes in Tara's sense of community. Do they fit with any of the 'desires for community' discussed in the previous section? Are they different in any way? If so, how?

Extract 3.1

TARA: People seem to take pride in their homes, they are concerned about their yards [gardens]. It's like an old-fashioned neighborhood where everyone knew everyone, but it's not to the point where everyone is a busybody and into everyone else's business. We had many opportunities to move, and I'm just so frightened that I could never find something like this because Lilly [her daughter] knows everybody in the neighborhood, and I know that if anyone saw her, if, you know, a construction worker or somebody was talking with her, I know that in a heartbeat they would call me or ask Lilly what she was up to. It is just like the old-fashioned neighborhoods we grew up in, where people know everyone.

Low, 2003, p. 59

Comment

It is possible here to trace elements of 'restoration' and 'security' desires for community, with Tara talking about 'old-fashioned neighbourhoods' in which everyone knows everyone else and looks out for them. This neighbourliness produces a sense of security, especially about the risks that Tara's daughter might face. This view of the 'old-fashioned neighbourhood' also implies a conception of sociality – involving a fine balance where people know 'everyone else', but stop short of being busybodies. Finally, there is a sense of solidarity – that people look out for one another – even if this is something less than community as a vehicle for collective mobilisation.

Other interviews in Low's study reveal a more complex or ambivalent relationship to the world of the gated community. For example, Extract 3.2 explicitly links living in such communities to the desire for security (and the fear of crime specifically), but Polly raises doubts about whether the community provides a satisfactory solution.

Activity 3.3

Read Polly's account in Extract 3.2 below and then look back at the extract from Tara. What is different in Polly's account?

Extract 3.2

POLLY: I think it really mattered to my husband, just for the security. [...] I think he's a little overboard when it comes to the fear factor ... just crime in general ... I certainly feel safe here because it's gated. It's not that I [don't] feel ambivalent, but I really like all this luxury. The one thing that's really striking is that you don't get door-to-door solicitors.

...

Sometimes [the security guards are] stiff, sometimes they're totally lax ... It's a hit-or-miss thing. Believe me, if you wanted to get into a gated community you could.

...

... Fear of crime, gangs, it's really out of proportion [...] I just feel that the crimes that people are afraid of here – kidnappings and drive-by shootings – they don't happen here. Those are segregated in their own residential communities. It's happening over there. So I believe that fear is probably the biggest factor why people live in gated communities.

Low, 2003, pp. 120–1

Comment

To me, it is interesting that Polly both talks about 'feeling safe' and liking 'all this luxury', but at the same time distances herself from other people's (including her husband's) fears about crime. This is a *comment* on the desire for security, rather than an *expression* of such a desire. We see some of the tensions of living in a security-controlled environment. In particular, security is never perfect and may even be frustrating.

These are just two of the many interviews on which Low's study is based. She is particularly interested in the *paradox of security* (and of community) in which the process of creating 'gated communities' produces its own spiral of problems – the frustrations described by Polly; doubts about the quality of the security; anxieties about the security guards; the fear of 'unknown' people entering the community – and a greater anxiety about the rest of society beyond the gates. In reading the following discussion, you should think about the paradoxes produced by this process of creating community. Low argues that gated communities are

> redefining the meaning of 'community' to include protective physical boundaries that determine who is inside and who is outside. In the 1940s and 1950s, 'community' referred to groups of people defined geographically, by where they live and work. But during the 1960s and 1970s, these place-based definitions broke down as social groups – associations, ethnic or religious affiliations, race and gender – increasingly became the basis of social and cultural identification and urban neighborhoods became more heterogeneous. A location-based definition, one that includes walls and gates, but also the desire for the social homogeneity of an earlier era, is reemerging.

> Gated community residents are interested in 'community', but a specific kind of community that includes protecting children and keeping out crime and others while at the same time controlling the environment and the quality of services. The 'community' they are searching for is one imagined from childhood or some idealized past. In a variety of ways, these residents are all searching for their version of the perfect community, one where there is no fear, no crime, no kidnapping, no 'other' people, where there is a reassuringly consistent architectural and physical landscape, amenities and services that work, and great neighbors who want exactly the same things.

> Gated community residents use gates to create the community they are searching for. But their personal housing decisions have had unintended societal consequences. Most important, they are

disruptive of other people's ability to experience 'community': community in the sense of an integration of the suburb and the city, community in terms of access to public open space, and community within the American tradition of racial and ethnic integration and social justice.

Architecture and the layout of towns and suburbs provide concrete, anchoring points of people's everyday life. These anchoring points reinforce our ideas about society at large. Gated communities and the social segregation and exclusion they materially represent make sense of and even rationalize problems Americans have with race, class, and gender inequality and social discrimination. The gated community contributes to a geography of social relations that produces fear and anxiety simply by locating a person's home and place identity in a secured enclave, gated, guarded, and locked.

(Low, 2003, pp. 230–1)

Low makes visible the way in which the movement to gated communities is dominated by desires for restoration and security – the return to 'the social homogeneity' of place associated with an earlier era, and where crime can be kept out.

In the following section you will look in more detail at the history of community and the ideas of social order with which it has been associated. In the US context, Low points to the ways in which community has been used to construct an idea of how people and place fit together: the search for places occupied by socially homogeneous groups, or 'people like us'. She draws out two paradoxes of this search for community: one internal to the gated community, the other external. Internally, she suggests that this way of achieving security itself creates 'fear and anxiety', projected on to the world beyond the gates as a threat to the 'secured enclave'. Gated communities *amplify* the fears and anxieties that led to people wanting to live within them in the first place. Externally, she argues that gated communities impact on the lives of those beyond the gates. By privatising and enclosing part of the public world, such communities disrupt other possibilities of living together and other meanings of community. In the process, inequalities of 'race, class and gender' are reproduced and institutionalised in the construction of spaces for 'people like us'. Models of social integration and social justice are refused in the defence of narrow interests. Community works through a dynamic of inclusion and exclusion, and gated communities offer a very sharp example of the social and spatial dynamics of ways in which people and place can be organised.

4 Imagining community?

As you have seen in earlier chapters, the idea of community blurs issues of place and shared interests or identities: those things that 'we' have in common. The quotation from Low towards the end of the preceding section drew attention to the way in which gated communities seem to draw on 'real' or 'imagined' ideals of community from an earlier era. In these ideals, Low suggests, there is a happy conjunction between people and place – neighbourhoods (the place) were relatively socially homogeneous (the people sharing a way of life, a social position or a set of values). In this section, I explore some of the images of community from earlier periods that inform our current enthusiasm for building or rebuilding communities. I will highlight three images of community:

1   the 'organic' community of rural society

2   the industrial community

3   the community in colonial governance.

Each of these contributes something distinctive to contemporary desires for and debates about community. Looking at all three together might also help us to see some of the contemporary paradoxes and problems associated with popular and political desires for community.

The first image emerges in the distinction between the country and the city (or the rural and the urban), associated with Tönnies' (1955) distinction between *Gemeinschaft* and *Gesellschaft* discussed in Chapter 1. Here community denotes an integrated and intimate set of social relationships different from the atomised and anonymous relationships that characterise modern urban society. In this view, communities are stable ways of living, held together by a shared way of life and a common culture. As Chapter 1 indicated, such images of community are still used to describe village life in the twenty-first century. They also provide a potent basis for critiques of 'modern living', identifying a sense of *lost* order, stability and continuity. In a major study of English ideas of the country and the city, Williams argued that this sense of loss recurs across history. As mentioned briefly in Section 2, he noted that each era looks back to a lost golden age:

> there is still a crisis of perspective. When we moved back in time, consistently directed to an earlier and happier rural England, we could find no place, no period, in which we could seriously rest ... And then what seems to be an old order, a 'traditional' society, keeps appearing, reappearing, at various bewildering dates: in practice as an idea, to some extent based in experience, against which contemporary change can be measured.
>
> (Williams, 1985, p. 35)

Williams's suggestion here is an important one: that the idea of community and its golden age provides a way of talking – a vocabulary – for discussing processes and problems of social change. I will pick up this theme again, but there are two other important points to draw out about this organic rural conception of community. The first concerns its conception of *social order.*

The image of social order associated with this organic rural idea of community is centred on stability. The community's way of life preserves tradition, habit and custom. The emphasis is on shared values, orientations and expectations. As a result, change is viewed as dangerous and threatening. It is typically treated as the result of 'outside influences': referring especially to people who are not 'from here', or not 'like us'. In Chapter 1, for example, the rural case study extracts identified 'people from the city' as being responsible for policies and attitudes that damaged the imagined stability and order of the rural way of life. For many, such stability is desirable, especially – as Williams (1985) argues – when set against the unsettling dynamics of social change that create instability and uncertainty. But, as the example of gated communities suggests, trying to create and sustain such order and stability is not without its costs and risks.

Activity 3.4

Why might trying to maintain a stable social order prove difficult? Think back to Low's discussion of gated communities in the previous section and make a note of points about the paradoxical consequences of securing community.

Comment

Low's discussion of gated communities suggests that maintaining a stable social order might be difficult due to:

■ a costly system of exclusion and controlled access, associated with a fear of 'others' and outsiders

■ the separation of the world into 'inside' and 'outside' the community

■ the relationship of such communities to patterns of social inequality (what sorts of people can afford to be 'included' in gated communities, and who gets 'excluded'?).

We might add some other points about this model of organic and stable community more generally:

■ The norms of conduct that ensure social order tend to be powerful and powerfully enforced.

- ■ 'Deviance' leads to punishment, social exclusion or expulsion.

- ■ Rural communities were built on, and sustained profound social inequalities of, both gender (in which 'traditional' societies meant 'traditional' families and a 'traditional' gendered division of labour) and class.

This last point directs us to the second issue about the organic rural community: the *social relations* of its social order. Such communities were, historically, built on profound inequalities – those living in the same place (the village) lived in very different conditions. Williams offers this account of an eighteenth-century English 'open field' village:

> There are three hundred souls. Of these, nearly two hundred are cottagers and labourers and their families, indoor servants, and the unattached poor – widows, orphans, the aged. Some seventy are the copyhold tenant farmers and their families. Some twenty are the freehold farmers and their families. The ten or twelve others are the squire and his family and the parson and his family ... There are, in effect, three classes: the gentry, the small entrepreneurs, the unpropertied poor. The inequalities of condition which the village contains and supports are profound and nobody, by exercise of sentiment, can convert it into a 'rural democracy' or, absurdly, a commune.
>
> (Williams, 1985, p. 102)

Ideas of integrated and organic village communities derived from a rural past conceal the social relations on which they were founded, and the associated social hierarchies that they sustained. Conceptions of stability and social order derived from this rural past were, in part, based on systems of inequality, power and deference (to the squire and the parson, for example). As a result, the social order was one in which 'people knew their place' and kept to it. Appeals to tradition, stability and social order thus have an ambivalent relationship to questions of inequality and power. They rarely name them as the desired features of community, but they are often critical features of what is meant by social order. Studies of more recent rural communities have pointed to their contradictory character, in which social orders of inequality and power are cross-cut by relationships of mutuality, solidarity and support among neighbours (Neal and Walters, 2008), while inequalities of positions of power are reflected in the traditions of radical politics and contested social relations that are also features of rural histories (e.g. Bell and Newby, 1972) and rural areas (e.g. Cloke and Little, 1997; Neal and Agyeman, 2006).

Figure 3.3
Working-class
community?

Our images of community do not derive solely from this organic rural tradition. They also have roots in more recent urban and industrial history in which ideas of 'working-class community' have been significant. In towns or areas of cities that were dominated by one industry, dense neighbourhoods developed whose inhabitants shared work, leisure and politics. Elaborate kinship networks connected people, and their fate was shaped by the shifting of an industry, or even a single employer. Sociologists and social anthropologists explored such working-class communities associated with coal mining, shipbuilding, deep-sea fishing, vehicle assembly and the dock work of East London (e.g. Dennis et al., 1956; Frankenberg, 1966; Young and Willmott, 1957; see also Critcher, 1979). Community here was characterised by a *shared* economic and social position, and by forms of familial, local and occupational solidarity, expressed in the image of people 'looking out for one another'. Such studies emphasised the dense and mutually supportive patterns of values and interaction that sustained people in these 'communities of fate'. They emphasised cultures or ways of life often ignored or denigrated in official knowledge of the post-Second World War period, when both central and local government were concerned to modernise the British way of life. For example, Young and Willmott's (1957) study of the East End revealed how the combination of work changes and rehousing were disrupting and dislocating forms of working-class family and community life.

Like the rural image of community, these ideas of urban–industrial community pose some difficult questions about both the social order and the social relations they describe. Typically, they contrast a stable, integrated and coherent social order within the community to an external world of threats and challenges. This contrast ignores dynamics and tensions within the communities themselves. Like the rural communities discussed above, these working-class communities appealed to a shared sense of values and could enforce norms of conduct in a ruthless manner – not least in terms of gender norms and sexuality. Gender relations were central to the working of these communities – with a strong 'traditional' distinction between the male world of work and the female world of home and family. Studies such as those mentioned varied in how visible they made 'women's work'. Some focused on the public world of work, politics and leisure dominated by men and male institutions (the working men's club, the pub, and so on). Others celebrated the role played by women – as mothers, daughters, grandmothers, sisters – in maintaining the webs of connection, interdependence and support that provided the fabric of community. None challenged this model of a division of labour, nor paid much attention to those places in which working-class women worked in paid employment as well as in the home (McDowell and Massey, 1984). This is part of a wider question about whether such 'communities' were ever typical of working-class life in Britain (Clarke, 1984; Critcher, 1979).

Figure 3.4

Street Scene (1935) by L.S. Lowry. Oil on canvas

More troublingly, such studies of working-class communities treated the question of class as a matter of occupation (these were 'manual workers') rather than as a matter of social relations. The other classes, such as those identified by Williams (1985), for example, are absent. The owners, proprietors and managers who organise and direct the work of these workers seem to live elsewhere and not to be part of the social relations of British capitalism of the period. Occasionally, such studies take up a colloquial distinction in working-class speech between 'us' (the class, the community, 'people like us') and 'them' – but 'they' designates an amorphous set of people who have and hold power of different sorts. 'They' might be owners, politicians, aristocrats, bureaucrats in local government, managers and more – but they are not part of any clearly articulated class relations. The only class that is *visible* is the working class.

Even when such studies were being conducted, there was a sense that they might be describing 'ways of life' under pressure from social changes. They overlapped in time, for example, with studies of the emerging privatised, affluent and mobile worker of the car industries (Goldthorpe et al., 1968; Zweig, 1961). Life in Luton, Dagenham or Linwood differed in crucial respects from the image of working-class community. Despite this, the image of the community – densely inhabited, mono-industrial and mono-cultural – persists to inform contemporary debates and desires. It offers an ideal of unity and stability – the coherence of people and place – that remains intimately associated with our contemporary interest in community, as we shall see in the following section.

Finally, our current understandings of community are also shaped by the history of colonial governance. In the period of empire, community was one of the keywords for thinking about 'native populations', in Asia especially. Colonial rule in India and elsewhere always had to address the question of how to identify, categorise and manage the people of the colonies (Pandey, 2005). Broad racial and national categories – Indian, African, etc. – were not refined enough to separate out different manageable groups for the purposes of governing. So, differences were identified and categorised – sometimes building on, and reinforcing, pre-existing differences of place, culture, religion and status, or even inventing such distinctions. We have inherited many terms from such colonial rule: tribes, castes, cultures and – not least – communities (Pandey, 2006). These were all ways of distinguishing different groups among those to be ruled: they were terms that distinguished 'natives' from the colonial power. As Chapter 2 indicated, the idea of community continues to exercise a considerable power in the politics and policies of development (see also Creed, 2006).

Colonisers were the bearers of civilisation and modernity, while 'natives' were the bearers of culture and tradition. Pandey (2006, p. 258) argues that 'nationhood has been the mark of the modern, what all great countries and people have achieved. Community is what existed before'. Colonised nations, in contrast, had not achieved nationhood, but were 'seen as social/political orders constituted by community or group ties as much as (if not more than) by individual interests' (Pandey, 2006, p. 258). Anthropology emerged as the study of 'ways of life', documenting the values, practices and cultures of these different groups. The development of anthropology – and its favoured methodology, ethnography – centred on the in-depth study of particular locales (such as villages) through participant observation and conversation. The aim was to both record and analyse the cultures of different social groups. The study of villages, communities and localised groupings aimed to explore 'others' from the vantage point of European civilisation, and was intertwined with the processes of a colonial rule. Such studies both accumulated scientific knowledge about the diversity of human cultures and informed colonial rulers about the people that they ruled.

Such differences and distinctions between tribes, castes, cultures and communities were integral to the processes of 'divide and rule' by which European colonisers managed their colonies. The idea of communities, in this context, referred to particular sorts of unities of people and place: communities were marked by a shared or common culture. As we have seen with other uses of the word 'community', the stress here was on internal stability and a shared tradition. Communities – for example, the Hindu, Muslim and Sikh communities of colonial India – were understood as a source of stability: they integrated their members into a 'way of life' and a 'sense of belonging'. But they were also a source of strain and problems for colonial governance, since dividing populations in this way could lead to intercommunal tensions and violence, most manifest in the process of partition – on 'communal' grounds of religion – associated with Indian independence. This conception of intercommunal tensions was also a central part of British images of Northern Ireland as divided between 'the two communities', a term that referred to both religious differences between Catholic and Protestant and their expected alignment with political orientations towards republican/nationalist and unionist politics respectively.

Like the rural and urban–industrial conceptions of community, this colonial image also contains key issues about social order and social relations. Social order is maintained both within communities (by traditional norms and values) and in the relations between them. Government stands *outside and above* the field of communities, providing the framework to enable communities to reconcile their differences. So, colonial governments simultaneously invented and

Figure 3.5
Governing
intercommunal
violence? Circa 1946:
British infantryman
standing guard at
Islamic bookshop in a
predominantly Hindu
area after bloody rioting
between Hindus and
Muslims on the eve of
Independence

enforced these categories of community and claimed to stand outside
intercommunal tensions. As the representatives of 'civilisation', colonial
governors administered and adjudicated between the different 'native
communities'. It is important to stress that in the emphasis on culture,
ethnicity or religion as the formative material of communities, we lose
sight of other social relations – of inequalities, of power differences, of
gendered divisions, for example. So, inequalities between colonisers and
local people are not visible in this view of society as a field of community
differences; and neither are class differences between local entrepreneurs,
landowners and officials, and the urban or rural poor (Sharma, 2008).

Activity 3.5

In what ways might our contemporary interest in community be shaped by these histories of community as a *rural* idea, as an *urban–industrial* idea and as a *colonial* idea?

Comment

I can think of at least five ways in which these histories have consequences for our current concern with community. We make use of ideas about community that:

■ treat place as the basis for common identities or ways of life (in village or urban–industrial settings)

■ emphasise the importance of shared values, orientations or traditions

■ refer to common religious, cultural, ethnic or racial identifications

■ identify multiple communities or cultures, and relations between them, as needing to be managed or regulated by governments

■ assume a natural (and historical) coherence of types of people and place (the partition of India at independence being an early example of trying to create places that were ethnically, communally and culturally coherent).

As you will see in the following section, these points play a vital part in conflicts over community in the present.

5   Contesting community?

Community has been revitalised as a keyword in popular and political discussions about social change and social order. As the previous chapters indicated, communities are seen as a solution to problems of social disorder of various kinds. But the current conditions for ideas of community differ in many ways from the earlier histories, in part because the social context of community talk has been changing. It may be helpful to draw out four sets of changes that – at the least – place new demands and pressures on the possibilities of creating or sustaining communities.

First, different sorts of mobility have unsettled *place* as the basis for community. For example, the increased mobility of industry and capital investment has shattered the connections between place and work, while the greater social and spatial mobility of people disperses people to new locations. As a result, places get 'reinvented' with new economies, new inhabitants and new sets of social relationships. The connections between people and places are more unsettled, fragile and contingent than our historical images of community could accommodate. As a result, questions of where people belong, or feel they belong, have become more complicated.

Second, social *heterogeneity* has increased: that is, societies are composed of more differentiated groups, in terms of class (economic differences between rich and poor have grown remarkably since 1980 in the UK), culture, lifestyle and ethnicity. This different social mix – and the increasing visibility of such heterogeneity – may make community both less and more significant. Community may be less significant and less possible if it requires social homogeneity (remember Low's comments on US neighbourhoods), or it may be that these differences become the basis for the formation of more communities (wealthy communities, the gay community, minority ethnic communities, and so on). As Chapter 1 suggested, *culture*, rather than place, has become increasingly important in identifying and defining communities.

Third, governments now expect individuals, families and communities to do more to secure their own welfare and well-being. As a consequence, the communities to which people are attached become both a resource and competitors for scarce public resources (investment, housing, and so on). Both Chapter 2 and Chapter 4 in this book point to some of the contentions around community in such policy fields. As you will see, questions of *belonging* – who belongs to specific communities and to whom do communities (and their resources) belong – become increasingly important.

Fourth, these changes involve a combination of mobility, inequality, vulnerability and insecurity that has become expressed in what we might call 'community talk' (as in Williams's (1985) discussion of social change and golden ages). In both political and popular discourses, 'community' has become a way of discussing social change, its consequences, its problems and its disorders. Images of community both speak of a golden age (before the current turbulence) and promise a better future in which order might be recreated, stability restored and insecurity controlled in ways that might enable people to live better lives.

Some of these problems about community are central to a recent study by Dench et al. (2006), which revisits the East End of London studied by Young and Willmott in the 1950s (Young and Willmott, 1957). The recent study identifies the East End as a place of intense *racial*

Figure 3.6
London Docklands
between the wars

antagonism, particularly over the provision and distribution of 'social housing'. In an article summarising the study, Geoff Dench and Kate Gavron argued:

> That simmering racial tension between the white working class and the large Bangladeshi community in Tower Hamlets has existed for more than 30 years is indisputable. But while conventional liberal opinion has tended to attribute its causes to white racism, the truth is far more complex.
>
> The story of racial conflict in the East End is part economic, part political, part historical. But what is most striking is the sense in which it is the direct, if unintended, consequence of well-meaning welfare policy – particularly in the area of social housing allocation.
> (Dench and Gavron, 2006)

Dench et al. interviewed people living in the East End, and present many examples of social welfare being seen as the focus of such racialised antagonism:

> The government makes the race problem by just giving them everything and us nothing. (Secretary living with husband and teenage children)
>
> I'm not happy with immigrants. We've got more than our fair share. The housing situation will never be solved. All the new houses are for immigrants. Big houses for big Pakistani families. They're officially not working, so they don't pay the rent. It is asking for racist trouble.

They're moving in everywhere. They come to take advantage of our social security. They break our laws – with teenagers pregnant by old men, and more than one wife. This is England! I think it will boil over. (Retired bank manager)

(Quoted in Dench et al., 2006, pp. 217–8)

The focus on questions of welfare policy out of the many economic and social changes that have affected the East End since the 1950s is a striking feature of this study. Dench et al. observe that the welfare system seemed to have changed to one that 'gave generously to those who put nothing into the pot, while making ordinary working people who did contribute feel like recipients of charity when drawing their entitlements' and a system where 'need is allowed to over-ride rights and claims arising out of an earlier, more directly exchange-based welfare state ethic' (Dench and Gavron, 2006). Welfare states have indeed been changing (Clarke, 2004; Dwyer, 2000). In the case of the UK, the move to a more conditional, targeted and residual welfare system, which was intended to encourage people to 'take responsibility for their own well-being', dramatically reduced the provision of social housing (see also Watt, 2006).

But systems of welfare provision, and especially social housing, have changed partly because of earlier struggles for social welfare and social justice. Social housing was itself the focus of extensive *anti-racist* struggles precisely because 'earned entitlements' and their implementation were discriminatory, privileging length of residence over need. Bangladeshis and other minority ethnic groups, together with allies in political parties and trade unions, campaigned to change housing policy and practice (Jones, 2006; Keith, 2006; Neveu, 1993).

Dench et al.'s *The New East End* is an important study in a number of ways. In this context, I want to link it to questions arising from the earlier sections of this chapter, asking how the idea of community is used; how questions of belonging are addressed; and what sort of social relations are made visible. Let us first look more closely at how ideas of community are used.

The word 'community' is sometimes applied to both groups being discussed: 'white and Bangladeshi communities had opposed interests over housing' (Dench and Gavron, 2006, p. 2). But more often the distinction is made between the 'Bangladeshi community' and the 'white working class': a juxtaposition that differentiates (ethnicity versus class) and implicitly privileges those who are identified as 'working class'. We might ask why are Bangladeshis not referred to as the Bangladeshi working class or the migrant working class? As you saw in the previous section, a strange view of class often appears in community studies. The study by Dench et al. consistently talks about

Figure 3.7
Redeveloped
Docklands: Canary
Wharf, 2005

this 'white working class', despite the fact that its introduction reflects on the dramatically changing composition of the East End in class terms, with the expansion of the City, the processes of gentrification and the appearance of a cosmopolitan middle class (Dench et al., 2006, pp. 19–23). The authors do refer regularly to a 'national elite' – meaning mainly politicians and liberal professionals – who have 'supported Bangladeshi interests in local conflicts over resources' (Dench et al., 2006, p. 219). But class relations in any larger sense are invisible in this study. At the same time, many of the white respondents identified by the authors have or have held occupations that are not obviously working class (from taxi drivers to publicans to bank managers). This gives a sort of 'working-class gloss' to the white respondents while denying a class location or identity to the Bangladeshis (see, in contrast, the discussion in Neveu, 1993, pp. 164–66, 283–4).

Meanwhile, Bangladeshis are treated as a coherent and consistent community, where other ethnographies have explored tensions and divisions. For example, a study undertaken in Spitalfields during the 1980s argued that there were different voices within the Bangladeshi community and that 'opposition to homogeneous, or homogenising visions of the "community" is certainly not new … The control exercised by the first generation of migrants and its hegemonic wish to be the unique voice of the "community" … have often been rejected' (Neveu, 1993, p. 298; quotation translated from the original French by John Clarke). This suggests something less than a unified and singular Bangladeshi community; rather, it points to a social group characterised by significant cultural, social and political divisions. But – as you have already seen in this book – the image of community tends to obscure internal divisions, distinctions and differences, and presents instead a unified and united entity.

In *The New East End* study, community plays a double role – moving between ideas of community as culture/ethnicity and community as place/locality. Increasing competition for council-provided housing, and its allocation on principles of need rather than historic residence, 'also had the effect of breaking up long-established East End family and community links' by failing to give priority to 'applicants with local and community connections' (Dench and Gavron, 2006, p. 2). Here the 'community' is both *local* and *historical*: people and place are viewed as tied together over generations. History links the East End's celebrated place in the Second World War (the docks serving as Britain's lifeline; and being the focus of intensive civilian bombing) and the promise of social reconstruction after the war. Many of Dench et al.'s interviewees connect this conception of *belonging* and *entitlement* to a sense of 'broken promises':

> We did our war service and now they do not want to know us. But if you are an immigrant you get the top brick off the chimney. (Retired driver)

> Let us have some priorities. Our parents fought a war for us. When the Bengalis come here they get full pensions. My wife has just been informed after years of paying full contributions she will only get a [small] pension when she retires. Why do they get it when they've contributed nothing? (Publican)

> Old people now are scrimping and saving. They don't get half of what they should get. Those who fought in the war would turn in their graves if they knew that Asians were getting everything. Years ago when you had lots of kids you had to support yourself. Now the state keeps you. (Market trader)
>
> (Quoted in Dench et al., 2006, pp. 215–6)

In a different study of East London undertaken in the mid 1990s, Georgie Wemyss (2006, p. 228) argued that 'white, working-class people were normalised as being the natural and historically legitimate occupiers of East End spaces in the discourses of the local and national media. They were at the top of the "hierarchy of belonging"'. This conception of belonging was constructed through identifying local histories stretching back across generations (Wemyss, 2006, p. 228). By contrast, Bangladeshi migrants and their descendants appear to be without a history: they are in, but not of, the locality and cannot belong to this version of community. Having a 'history' validates the connection of 'race' and place. 'Localness' simultaneously expresses and

Figure 3.8
A multi-ethnic
community?

denies a racialised understanding of community and belonging. Gail Lewis (2000) has called this the 'now you see it, now you don't' flickering character of racism in contemporary Britain. Dench and Gavron argue that:

> The system has tended to treat with scorn Bethnal Greeners' 'irrational' attachment to their locality. Arguably, there has been an 'anti-racist card' played against the white working class. The response of planners to white anxieties around housing, has been to dismiss the idea of locality, and to expect people to exercise their housing entitlements elsewhere if necessary. When local white residents have objected, their assertions of local commitment have been made to look unreasonable by the suggestion that what they are objecting to really is that the Bangladeshis competing with them are not white.
> (Dench and Gavron, 2006, p. 2)

We might think about how the meanings of community make it possible for *both* these things to be true simultaneously. 'Community' expresses a complex connection between people and place. The 'white working class' belong to the place – and, in turn, expect the place to belong to them. They are the 'Bethnal Greeners'. By contrast, Bangladeshis are a community of culture/ethnicity, but are 'out of place' and do not 'belong' to the East End. This means that, as a result, some may claim that the East End – and its public resources – does not, and should not, belong to them.

Activity 3.6

Stop for a moment and make a note of the different ideas of belonging and community that are visible in this discussion. Why might they be in tension?

Comment

The New East End study raises difficult questions about what community means – since it mingles community as place/locality and community as culture/ethnicity. The idea of the 'white working class' combines culture/ethnicity and place in an image of belonging. The 'Bangladeshi community' is only a community of culture/ethnicity and cannot 'belong' to the locality. Instead of belonging, it is marked by a sense of 'entitlement' through needs or rights, in relation to welfare and housing in particular.

Culturally and politically, both groups have mobilised ideas of community in relation to questions of belonging and entitlement and to ideas of citizenship. But they involve very different sorts of claims – and these are claims on *shrinking* resources: on territory, social welfare and social housing in particular. To whom should these public resources belong, and on what conditions?

There is a case for situating the current politics of community in wider contexts that help to explain the contemporary tensions around place, 'race'/ethnicity and belonging. We can then see the role of community as a keyword through which such changes are reflected and debated. Such contexts include the turbulent relations between changing welfare states, growing inequalities and the increasingly troubled question of national identity and belonging (see Clarke, 2004). Don Kalb (2005, p. 197) suggests that social policy and forms of social provision have 'been locked into increasingly defensive, under-funded, local and parochial conditions'. He also argues that the pressures of globalising processes of economic and political change have 'invited an upsurge of counter-narratives of nationalism, localism, religion and tradition ... The dynamics of cultural closure ... got an extra push from increasing competition for scarce resources in land, labor, housing, education and sometimes marriage markets' (Kalb, 2005, p. 187). London's East End might be regarded as one of the places in which such tensions and pressures become compressed as mobilities, inequalities and insecurities come up against 'counter-narratives of nationalism, localism, religion and tradition'. The East End is by no means unique in this respect: many other places face equally conflict-ridden and disturbing processes. The East End, however, is marked by a discourse of community – and communities – as a way of talking about social change and social (dis)order. It may be worth returning to the observation by Williams, which I quoted earlier:

> And then what seems an old order, a 'traditional' society, keeps appearing, reappearing at various bewildering dates: in practice as an idea, to some extent based in experience, against which contemporary change can be measured. The structure of feeling within which this backward reference is to be understood is not then primarily a matter of historical explanation and analysis. What is really significant is this particular kind of reaction to the fact of change, and this has more real and more interesting social causes.
>
> (Williams, 1985, p. 35)

Like Williams's rural 'old order', the 'community' of the East End of London also shifts in time. When Young and Willmott (1957) were engaged in their study of Bethnal Green in the 1950s, the golden age was already in the past – challenged by new processes of rehousing, welfare policies and economic development. It is hard to pin down exactly when in the East End's long and turbulent – and immigration driven – history the golden age of the stable, unified and white working class took place (see, for example, Stedman-Jones, 1971, 1984). Presumably it was not during the Depression (and the fascist movements) of the 1930s. Nor would it be obviously identified with the Victorian era, characterised by earlier waves of immigration, violence, intense poverty and class conflict, although it is undoubtedly true that the rise and prestige of the London docks (and dock work) was intimately related to the reach of empire. We may do better, as Williams suggests, to treat golden age stories as ways of reflecting on, and trying to deal with, disorderly and unsettling dynamics of social change in the present. 'Community' provides a language for imagining a better world of either past or future – but it is a language in which questions of inclusion and exclusion, belonging, attachment and entitlement are absolutely central.

6   Review

There are two key concerns to be addressed in reviewing this chapter. The first involves issues of evidence and analysis in the study of communities. The second involves trying to draw together the discussion of community, social change and social order. Let us turn first to the process of studying community because the chapter has made extensive use of two recent studies that exemplify some of the strengths and problems of researching communities. These studies overlap in methods, with interviewing residents a central feature of both (51 in the East End; 50 in the gated communities). The East End study by Dench et al. links this to a wider, more quantitative survey of the area's population, while Low's study of gated communities links interviewing to 'participant observation', living within such communities and spending time with residents in their everyday activities within and beyond the gates. Low's approach is closer to the traditional anthropological approach (ethnography) to studying communities, whereas Dench et al. aim to replicate the methods used in the Young and Willmott study of the 1950s.

In the end, the core claims made in both studies rest on the richness of the interviews. It is extracts from these interviews that carry the arguments being presented. They are, then, *qualitative* studies, trying to draw out the experiences, orientations and accounts of the people in the places being studied. Although they share this orientation, they differ in other respects. For me, the most important difference lies in how they deal with their evidence in relation to wider contexts and dynamics. Dench et al. tend to deal with the evidence as 'testimony': ordinary people talking about how life is, and how it got to be this way. They seem to see their role as 'giving voice' to voices that might not be heard otherwise. In particular, they want to bring us the voices of those that they identify as the 'white working class'. They are sympathetic listeners – appreciating the experiences and explanations being offered. Low is also a sympathetic listener, but deals with the evidence in a rather different way. She looks for the way in which the experiences, emotions and explanations being offered work in relation to larger contexts. She asks how people imagine community, how they try to create it, and what the consequences of those efforts are for larger social dynamics. She takes seriously the desires that people have for community, but asks challenging questions about the contexts, conditions and consequences of those desires. This is a persistently difficult issue for forms of qualitative social research: how far does the researcher accept and reproduce the terms of reference of those being studied; and how far does she or he contextualise them, ask questions about how they came to be this way, and raise issues about the consequences of this way of thinking and this way of life? It is a difficult issue because there is no easy way of settling these problems, but when reading qualitative studies, it is an important issue to keep in mind.

Finally, there is the question of how community is linked to social change and social order. Let me offer three summary points about these connections:

1 *Ideas of community always contain an image of social order:* a model of how life ought to be, how social relationships ought to be organised, and how people should conduct themselves. These images of social order are diverse – ranging from ideas about hierarchy and people 'knowing their place' to ideas of transparent or unmediated human interaction.

2 *Ideas of community are often a way of talking about social change:* providing a reference point for concerns about insecurity, unsettling changes, and experiences of dislocation and loss, as Williams suggests. 'Community talk' is one of the ways in which societies address change, especially changes in identity, belonging, authority and power.

3 *Ideas of community have questions of belonging at their centre:* who belongs to a community is one aspect of this – whether community is understood as a place or a culture. Community works on a dynamic of inclusion and exclusion. But there is a second question about *what belongs to people* because they are part of a community – access to common resources such as welfare benefits and services, for example. As you have seen, such questions of belonging bring together ideas of community as place and community as 'race' in difficult and contested ways.

It is the ways in which this 'community talk' and questions of social order and social change have come increasingly to inform crime control and social welfare policy development that are addressed by Gordon Hughes in the next chapter.

Further reading

Setha Low's *Behind the Gates* (2006, Routledge) is an exemplary study of a new form of community. Gated communities are to be found across the world, and Rowland Atkinson and Sarah Blandy's *Gated Communities* (2005, Routledge) provides detailed case studies from South America and South Africa, as well as from North America. Raymond Williams's *Keywords* (1976, Fontana) remains a vital resource for thinking about words and their social and political significance; it includes a lengthy entry on community. *Imagining Welfare Futures* (edited by Gordon Hughes, 1998, Routledge/The Open University) offers a thoughtful comparison between images of community, citizen and consumer in debates over welfare reform. The work of the Institute of Community Studies can be followed at the Michael Young Foundation website: http://www.youngfoundation.org.uk (Accessed 11 July 2008).

References

Bell, C. and Newby, H. (1972) *Community Studies: An Introduction to the Sociology of the Local Community*, London, HarperCollins.

Clarke, J. (1984) 'There's no place like ... cultures of difference' in Massey and Allen (eds) (1984).

Clarke, J. (2004) *Changing Welfare, Changing States: New Directions in Social Policy*, London, Sage.

Clarke, J. (2005) 'New Labour's citizens: activated, empowered, responsibilised, abandoned?', *Critical Social Policy*, vol. 25, no. 4, pp. 447–63.

Cloke, P. and Little, J. (eds) (1997) *Contested Countryside Cultures: Otherness, Marginalisation and Rurality*, London, Routledge.

Cochrane, A. and Talbot, D. (eds) (2008) *Security: Welfare, Crime and Society*, Maidenhead, Open University Press/Milton Keynes, The Open University.

Creed, G. (ed.) (2006) *The Seductions of Community: Emancipations, Oppressions, Quandaries*, Santa Fe, NM, School of American Research Press/Oxford, James Currey.

Critcher, C. (1979) 'Sociology, cultural studies and the post-war working class' in Clarke, J., Critcher, C. and Johnson, R. (eds) *Working Class Culture: Studies in History and Theory*, London, Hutchinson.

Dench, G. and Gavron, K. (2006) 'Lost horizons', *The Guardian*, 8 February 2006 [online], http://www.youngfoundation.org.uk/index.php?p=255 (Accessed 13 June 2006).

Dench, G., Gavron, K. and Young, M. (2006) *The New East End: Kinship, Race and Conflict*, London, Profile Books.

Dennis, N., Henriques, F. and Slaughter, C. (1956) *Coal is Our Life*, London, Eyre and Spottiswood.

Dwyer, P. (2000) *Welfare Rights and Responsibilities: Contesting Social Citizenship*, Bristol, The Policy Press.

Esping-Andersen, G. (1990) *The Three Worlds of Welfare Capitalism*, Cambridge, Polity Press.

Frankenberg, R. (1966) *Communities in Britain: Social Life in Town and Country*, Harmondsworth, Penguin.

Goldthorpe, J., Lockwood, D, and Platt, J. (1968) *The Affluent Worker: Volume 1*, Cambridge, Cambridge University Press.

Hughes, G. (2007) *The Politics of Crime and Community*, London, Palgrave.

Jewkes, Y. (2008) 'Insecurity, fear and social retreat' in Cochrane, A. and Talbot, D. (eds) *Security: Welfare, Crime and Society*, Maidenhead, Open University Press/Milton Keynes, The Open University.

Jones, C. (2006) 'New myths of the East End', *Socialist Review*, April [online], http://www.socialistreview.org.uk/article.php?articlenumber=9709 (Accessed 29 July 2007).

Kalb, D. (2005) 'From flows to violence: politics and knowledge in the debates on globalization and empire', *Anthropological Theory*, vol. 5, no. 2, pp. 176–204.

Keith, M. (2006) 'We should not confuse nostalgia with history', *The Guardian*, 7 March [online], http://society.guardian.co.uk/socialexclusion/comment/0,,1725408,00.html (Accessed 13 June 2006).

Lewis, G. (2000) *'Race', Gender, Welfare: Encounters in a Postcolonial Society*, Cambridge, Polity Press.

Low, S. (2003) *Behind the Gates: Life, Security and the Pursuit of Happiness in Fortress America*, New York and London, Routledge.

McDowell, L. and Massey, D. (1984) 'A woman's place?' in Massey and Allen (eds) (1984).

Massey, D. and Allen, J. (eds) (1984) *Geography Matters!*, Cambridge, Cambridge University Press.

Neal, S. and Agyeman, J. (2006) *The New Countryside? Ethnicity, Nation and Exclusion in Contemporary Rural Britain*, Bristol, The Policy Press.

Neal, S. and Walters, R. (2008) 'Rural be/longing and rural social organizations: conviviality and community-making in the English countryside', *Sociology*, vol. 42, no. 2, pp. 279–97.

Neveu, C. (1993) *Communauté, nationalité et citoyenneté. De l'autre côté du miroir: les Bangladeshis de Londres*, Paris, Éditions Karthala.

Pandey, G. (2005) *The Construction of Communalism in North India* (2nd edn), Oxford, Oxford University Press.

Pandey, G. (2006) 'The politics of community: some notes from India' in Creed, G. (ed.) *The Seductions of Community: Emancipations, Oppressions, Quandaries*, Santa Fe, NM, School of American Research Press/Oxford, James Currey.

Sennett, R. (2006) *The Culture of the New Capitalism*, Connecticut, NH, Yale University Press.

Sharma, A. (2008) *Empowerment Rules*, Minneapolis, MO, University of Minnesota Press.

Stedman-Jones, G. (1971) *Outcast London*, Oxford, Oxford University Press.

Stedman-Jones, G. (1984) *Languages of Class*, Cambridge, Cambridge University Press.

Studdert, D. (2005) *Conceptualising Community: Beyond the State and Individual*, Basingstoke, Palgrave Macmillan.

Tönnies, F. (1955) *Community and Association*, London, Routledge International Library of Sociology. (First published in German as *Gemeinschaft und Gesellschaft*, 1887.)

Watt, P. (2006) 'Respectability, roughness and "race": Neighbourhood place images and the making of working-class social distinctions in London', *International Journal of Urban and Regional Research*, vol. 30, no. 4, pp. 776–97.

Wemyss, G. (2006) 'The power to tolerate: contests over Britishness and belonging in East London', *Patterns of Prejudice*, vol. 40, no. 3, pp. 215–36.

Williams, R. (1976) *Keywords*, London, Fontana.

Williams, R. (1985) *The Country and the City*, London, The Hogarth Press.

Young, M. and Willmott, P. (1957) *Family and Kinship in East London*, London, Allen Lane.

Zweig, F. (1961) *The Worker in an Affluent Society*, London, Heinemann.

Chapter 4
Community safety and the governance of 'problem populations'

Gordon Hughes

Contents

1   Introduction

This chapter begins by defining the keywords in its title. It uses an activity, first to help unpack the meanings of these and, second, to introduce the main aims of the chapter and its contribution to the wider story of this book on 'community' and entanglements between policies of crime control and social welfare.

Activity 4.1

Think about the term 'community safety' – is it a familiar term? Have you heard it mentioned in your everyday life – at work, in bars, in clubs, at home, at school or in local policy debates reproduced in the media in your locality? What do you understand it to mean? Would you define it as a crime control or a social policy initiative?

Comment

'Community safety' remains a relatively little known term across much of the population, as you may find out yourself from talking to friends and relatives about the issues you will be reading about here. Community safety as a distinct field of public policy is a relatively new area of public service activity dating from the late 1980s in the UK. Unlike such terms as 'community policing' and 'community health', it is not yet present in the standard English dictionaries as a specific entry. Concerns over crime, disorder and antisocial behaviour are much more prominent in the popular imagination than that of community safety. Indeed, the latter in turn is often understood narrowly as being synonymous with attempts at reducing crime, disorder and antisocial behaviour. Let us begin with a provisional working definition of community safety taken from *The Sage Dictionary of Criminology*:

> The strategy which seeks to move beyond a police-driven crime prevention agenda, to involve other agencies and generate greater participation from all sections of the 'community'. It has been particularly associated with local 'partnership' strategies of crime and disorder reduction from local authorities. However, it is a capacious phrase which may also refer to strategies aimed at improving community safety ... [by addressing] harms from all sources, not just those classifiable as 'crimes'.
>
> (Hughes, 2006, p. 54)

With this definition in mind, this chapter will examine community safety as a *hybrid* policy field; that is, it is designed to deliver policy simultaneously in relation to both crime control and social welfare.

What about the second part of the chapter's title? 'The governance of "problem populations"' aims to capture the processes by which communities and populations 'get' targeted in policy as people and places for intervention because they are perceived to be and/or are represented as both 'dangerous'/*a* risk and 'vulnerable'/*at* risk (see **Mooney, 2008**).

Activity 4.2

The chapter uses the term 'problem populations' as a means of understanding the nature of groups that are seen *as* 'problems' for community safety as a result of their behaviour, attitude and lifestyle, but which are viewed simultaneously as *having* 'problems' due either to, again, their own actions, or to the attitudes and behaviour of others. The usual way in which such groups are referred to in formal policy discourse is as 'hard-to-reach' groups. Look at one definition of 'hard-to-reach' groups as suggested in the official Home Office guidance that went out to all crime and disorder reduction partnerships (CDRPs) or community safety partnerships (CSPs) in 1998: 'young men, the homeless, drug users, the gay community, members of minority ethnic communities, children, those who suffer domestic abuse, and the elderly' (quoted in Cook, 2006, p. 127). What are the likely difficulties with such a loose definition?

Comment

On any count, this list of categories covers such a significant proportion of the population as to become meaningless. According to Dee Cook (2006, p. 127), the term is also dangerous in its 'othering' potential: 'The term "hard to reach" is both stigmatising and falsely assumes homogeneity among individuals within the groups so labelled.' Such individuals are often blamed in part for their own situation if they do not engage in education, paid work, training, effective parenting, and so on, with emphasis being placed on personal or communal responsibility rather than on structural factors. They are usually distinct from those members of the community to whom community safety appeals; that is, the 'normal' and 'law-abiding' majority (of consumers, workers and 'settled' familial members).

The list of candidates for 'problem populations' is clearly potentially wide ranging and, in contemporary policy terms, tends to include Travellers and Gypsies, people with mental health problems, offenders and ex-offenders, drug users, 'antisocial' youths, homeless or street people, migrants and asylum seekers, and sex workers. All these groups have been recipients of community safety policy and practice and, in turn, have been constructed as 'problems' needing both help and control. For the purposes of this chapter, I examine the specific case of Aboriginal or indigenous populations in contemporary Australia as a particularly telling example of 'dangerous' and 'vulnerable' communities, which have been subjected to processes of generally 'top-down' control via both social welfare and crime control policies and practices, often under the banner of 'crime prevention' or 'community safety'. This example also illustrates the transnational character of policy issues around local community safety in the contemporary world.

Let us now begin to join up these two working definitions that constitute the chapter title and the substantive concerns of what follows. Chapters 2 and 3 were concerned with the management and organisation of communities as sites of policy making and social order. The focus of this chapter continues with this overarching concern with the way in which communities are *manufactured* within policy and social order agendas.

Drawing on the example of the UK, Section 2 plots the rise and consolidation of community safety policy and practice. This discussion illustrates how and in what ways community safety as a site of 'community governance' may be understood as an exemplar for demonstrating the complex connections between social welfare and crime control. This section also explores the evaluation of this policy field in terms of its successes and limitations, drawing in particular on the contested evidence, both quantitative and qualitative, as to 'what works'. Following this, Section 3 then examines the ways in which community safety may be said to exemplify a site of 'community governance'. Section 4 focuses on populations and places which, in the field of community safety and crime control strategies, are constructed as 'a risk' and as 'at risk', through the example of the indigenous peoples of Australia, often termed collectively as 'Aboriginal communities'. This population is the object – both as victims *and* as perpetrators – of national and local community safety priorities to reduce violent crime, antisocial behaviour, alcohol and substance abuse, family and child abuse, and hate crime.

The aims of this chapter are to:

- examine the ways in which community safety has had significant consequences for the merging of social welfare policy and crime control in recent decades

- look at how evidence relates to community safety policymaking

- explore the policy consequences of the use of the term 'community' both to identify problem populations and as a basis for responding to these populations.

2 Criminal justice or social policy? Community safety as a 'hybrid' policy field

Community safety as a policy approach sits at the intersection of attempts by the state to deliver welfare and security *and* policing and control in local communities. Community safety emerged in the 1980s as a local governmental strategy that sought to move beyond the traditionally police-driven agenda of crime prevention. Apart from seeking to involve other 'social' agencies in crime prevention (i.e. moving from single- to multi-agency activities), community safety has also been associated with more aspirational claims both to generate greater participation, and possibly leadership, from all sections of the community, geographically defined, in crime prevention, and in targeting social harms from sources other than just those classifiable as 'crimes'. As a long-term outcome, community safety across the Western world is often linked in government discourse and policy aspiration to the 'communitarian'- and 'social capital'-oriented ambition of replacing fearful, insecure communities with 'responsibilised' safe and secure ones (see Chapter 1). In the national politics of the contemporary UK in the 1990s and 2000s, for example, it was a crucial component of the mantra 'tough on crime, tough on the causes of crime'. Once again, we see that community safety sits at the fault line of repressive crime control ('tough on crime') and more preventive and welfare strategies ('tough on the causes of crime').

Table 4.1 Defining crime reduction and crime prevention

Crime reduction	Crime prevention
Definition: At its simplest and most circular or tautological, crime reduction is any measure or variety of measures aimed at reducing crime. The term has become associated chiefly with targeted and relatively short-term situational and policing measures put in place by a variety of local agencies and in line with central government performance targets. More accurately in the contemporary UK context, crime reduction is an approach that gives primacy to technical and numerical measurement and the trappings of a 'scientific' evaluation of effectiveness.	*Definition:* Any action taken or technique employed by private individuals and groups or public agencies aimed at the prevention and reduction of damage caused by acts defined as criminal by the state. Given that crimes are events proscribed by legal statute, it is not surprising that there is a wide plethora of activities associated with the term.

Definitions of community safety – like that of 'crime prevention' and 'crime (and disorder) reduction' (see Table 4.1) – will always remain the subject of intense debate, given that crime is a socially and historically changing category. Crimes after all are actions prohibited by specific laws at particular times and in particular places. Few academic commentators would dissent from the starting point that there is no universally accepted definition of either community safety or crime prevention (Crawford, 2007). However, for the purposes of governance, community safety is associated largely with public actions aimed at a broad range of crimes and, increasingly, 'disorder' or acts of 'antisocial behaviour' and 'incivilities' in specific localities and communities (see Chapter 2). As noted above, at the more rhetorical level, community safety is a form of both crime prevention and safety promotion involving 'policing' in the broadest sense of the word, seeking the participation of community members alongside formal agencies of the local state and quasi-formal voluntary and private agencies. In this sense community safety is a clear example of the broad shift from 'government' to 'governance' noted by Allan Cochrane and Janet Newman (Chapter 2 in this volume).

2.1 The UK experiment in community safety

The last decades of the twentieth century witnessed a growing strain on the criminal justice system. The combined crisis of the criminal justice system's and welfare state's responses to crime and disorder was captured by the following indicators:

- the increasing rate of recorded crime and the numbers of people passing through the different parts of the system

- overload combined with a crisis of efficiency (e.g. the declining clear-up rates of the police, overloaded courts and the overcrowding of prisons)

- a growing awareness of the extensive social and economic costs of crime; and, crucially, the increasing recognition that formal processes of criminal justice (i.e. detection, apprehension, prosecution, sentencing and punishment of offenders) have only a limited effect on controlling crime (Hughes and McLaughlin, 2002).

In response to the widespread acknowledgement of this crisis of both state welfare and criminal justice, two preventive ways of thinking, or 'logics', have come to the fore since the 1980s and become embedded in much of the work of local community safety partnerships (CSPs), namely situational crime prevention and social crime prevention (Hughes, 1998). These two logics capture a key problematic that remains at the heart of crime prevention practice: what Adam Crawford (1998) has termed the tension between reducing opportunities through situational measures as against social modes of intervention. Situational crime prevention chiefly concerns 'designing out' crime via opportunity reduction, such as the installation of preventive technologies like CCTV and 'alley gates' in both private and public spaces. Social crime prevention, on the other hand, is focused chiefly on changing targeted social environments and the motivations of offenders, and promoting 'community' development initiatives. Common to both elements of situational and social crime prevention is their claim to be both less damaging and more effective than traditional (reactive 'law and order') criminal justice approaches.

In the discussion that follows, the main features of the institutional context of community safety at the national level are outlined. It is difficult to deny from the outset that there has been a highly prescriptive and directive central government shaping of the contemporary preventive infrastructure in the UK. This is indicative of a 'sovereign' state strategy that stresses greater central control ('steering') alongside the diffusion of responsibility for the delivery of crime control ('rowing') to a wide array agencies and groups, both public and private, voluntary and statutory in character. For commentators like Nikolas Rose (1999), these developments are part of a broader movement towards enlisting communities as the new and preferred sites of governance (see also Chapters 1 and 2).

The emergence of community safety as a field of policy in the UK is most usefully viewed as the result of two interconnected features of government thinking, namely a political discourse of civic communitarianism and social capital, and a 'modernising' public management project. To give one example, as a result of the Crime and Disorder Act (CDA) 1998 in England and Wales, the aim to tackle disorder and antisocial behaviour through the establishment of exclusion orders, such as Child Curfew and Parenting and Anti-social Behaviour Orders, was a central feature of this fused communitarian and public management project. It is important to note how moral or social transgressions, as well as law breaking, came under the scope of the communitarian-inspired powers vested in local crime and disorder reduction partnerships (CDRPs) from the late 1990s. Such developments are illustrative of the entanglements and possible contradictions associated with control and welfare in the field of community safety. This ambitious national project, and programme of local policy implementation, was also structured by the development of a 'what works', evidence-based framework for crime and disorder reduction policy and practice (Section 2.2 discusses the nature of the evidence used to assess success and failure in this policy area).

What are the broad character of and powers associated with such CSPs? To get an initial view of their nature, let us examine the powers associated with what were termed CDRPs in England and CSPs in Wales in the decade immediately following the CDA 1998.

Between 1998 and 2007 all 376 of these statutory partnerships in England and Wales were legally obliged and empowered to:

- carry out audits of local crime and disorder problems

- consult with all sections of the local community

- publish three-year crime and disorder reduction strategies based on the findings of the audits

- identify targets and performance indicators for each part of the strategy, with specified timescales

- publish the audit, strategy and the targets

- report annually on progress against the targets.

Most CDRPs and CSPs show very similar organisational structures. For example: there is a formal strategic/operational division; there are usually specific thematic or geographically based 'action' teams; and the key statutory partners or 'responsible' authorities are made up of public agencies ranging from the local authority to police, police authority, probation, fire and health, alongside other agencies from both the statutory and voluntary sectors. The 'community' is usually presented in the local strategies as a spatial and moral concept, emphasising locality and belonging and unity (albeit across consensual diversity). However, there is also a common tendency to place certain groups outside the community due to their 'antisocial' activities, pointing to the key role of boundary and exclusion in representations of community. In turn, the community is usually 'passively' present in terms of being 'consulted' rather than an active participant in the planning and delivery of community safety.

There continue to be reforms of the work of the CDRPs as the vehicles for community safety in the UK, which seek to improve their performance. However, the work of CDRPs/CSPs as the institutional vehicles of community safety remains substantively determined by the central government agenda of targeted, 'evidence-based' and measurable crime and disorder reduction, linked to specific negotiated priorities.

Activity 4.3

Write a list of the types of crime, threats to safety and related harms that you think are the most threatening activities both to your own private safety and to public safety more generally in your locality. Restrict yourself to six priority areas.

Comment

The following priorities are taken from the published strategies of the twenty-two CSPs in Wales for 2005–08 and reflect the typical priorities shared across most partnerships in the UK. Note that the typical number of substantive priorities for local partnerships is usually about six in total:

- antisocial behaviour*

- arson

- burglary

- domestic abuse

- fear of crime*

- hate crime

- home safety

- prolific and persistent offenders

- property/business crime

- road safety

- rural crime

- substance abuse*

- vehicle crime

- violence

- youth offending.*

Those marked with an asterisk (*) were consistently among the top priorities in CSPs in Wales (see Edwards and Hughes, 2008a). How do the priorities listed above match your own list of priorities? What is the balance of crimes and non-criminalised 'harms'? Are 'welfare' issues likely to enter into the work associated with these policy priorities, or is the balance tipped in favour of crime control concerns?

The focus of CSPs in terms of their stated priorities is predominantly on crime and disorder reduction. On the surface this suggests that they are engaged primarily in local social control rather than in social policy work. However, the logic of such control work may be preventive rather than purely repressive and enforcement oriented (Edwards and Hughes, 2008b).

The centrally propelled and Home Office-directed development and institutionalisation of community safety is strikingly apparent across every local government authority in England and Wales (and increasingly across Scotland and Northern Ireland). Such processes have seen an ever-increasing number of multi-agency community safety teams – managers, officers, project workers, police secondees, 'drug action teams', Anti-social Behaviour Units – which form part, however uneasily, of local governmental structures and processes. Part of this is the policy recognition that effective crime control strategies must be rooted in the dynamics of local communities. With a policy and political focus on disorder and the antisocial, the UK government appears to be engaged in promoting highly localised crime control and welfare strategies especially targeted at 'problem' communities.

Figure 4.1
A satirical comment on community support officers from the political cartoonist Steve Bell

2.2 Success or failure? Weighing up the 'evidence' of the national community safety experiment

The aim of this part of the chapter is twofold, namely to discuss how the success or otherwise of CDRPs/CSPs as the institutional vehicles for crime and disorder reduction might be evaluated and, through this focus, to introduce various forms of social scientific evidence that may be deployed to assess 'what works' or 'what fails'.

You will be aware that social scientific evidence may be quantitative or qualitative. In previous chapters, the focus has been mainly on the qualitative. In the discussion here, the focus will be on the quantitative evidence that has been used to assess the performance of partnerships as public institutions aimed at crime and disorder reduction and the promotion of community safety. As is true across both the public and private sector, the dominant form of evidence used to assess performance in the field of community safety is statistical in nature. Accordingly, there are now statistically based league tables that rank local CDRPs/CSPs according to their proven success in reducing targeted priorities set by the CDRP/CSP in compliance with national targets, called public service agreements (PSAs). Let us now look at some of the evidence generated statistically about the crime reduction outcomes of CDRPs/CSPs.

Across England and Wales, all partnerships have been regularly monitored in terms of their performance in meeting reduction targets relative to six key areas of crime reduction, which in turn are derived from the statistical data generated by the national British Crime Survey (BCS). At the time of writing, there are six national comparators against which the performance of each CDRP/CSP is evaluated as either failing or successful. These are:

■ violence against the person

■ sex offences

■ robbery

■ burglary (dwelling)

■ theft of motor vehicle

■ theft from motor vehicle.

These selected categories are clearly not exhaustive of all crimes committed, nor are they indicators of safety, but they are used, pragmatically and perhaps problematically, by central government to assess success in this field. More broadly, this reflects the dominance of Treasury quantitative-driven calculations of how to measure public service performance.

Activity 4.4

You should now look at the statistical data in Table 4.2, which is taken from the Home Office website and contains extensive and detailed data on local CDRP/CSP performances. CDRPs/CSPs are grouped according to their police force area. Given the size of the Home Office data set, the data in Table 4.2 has been edited for the purposes of this chapter and gives information on only three of the six overall crime categories and for only one of each of the geographical locations.

It is important to note that those CDRPs/CSPs with a minus number are 'failing' to match what should be expected of them in terms of some basic comparisons regarding type of population and previous crime rates. How useful do you find this data in assessing the community safety work of CDRPs/CSPs? What are the limitations of this evidence for evaluating local outcomes in the field of community safety as against crime reduction?

Table 4.2 Crime and disorder reduction partnerships and community safety partnerships: recorded crime for three key offences and British Crime Survey comparator 2005–06 to 2006–07

Force	CDRP name	Population figures (thousands)	Household figures (thousands)	Violence against the person: offences recorded 05/06	Violence against the person: offences recorded 06/07	Violence against the person: change 05/06–06/07 (%)
Avon & Somerset	Bath and North East Somerset	174	73	2877	3000	4
Bedfordshire	Bedford	153	62	2451	2410	-2
Cambridgeshire	Cambridge	124	46	2009	2173	8
Cheshire	Chester	119	51	2536	2392	-6
Cleveland	Hartlepool	90	38	2919	2653	-9
Cumbria	Allerdale	96	41	1634	1476	-10
Derbyshire	Amber Valley	119	51	1764	1853	5
Devon & Cornwall	Caradon	82	35	920	884	-4
Dorset	Bournemouth	164	73	4892	4692	-4
Durham	Chester-le-Street	53	23	764	875	15
Dyfed-Powys	Carmarthenshire	178	76	2737	2824	3
Essex	Basildon	167	71	2162	2403	11
Gloucestershire	Cheltenham	112	49	2923	2765	-5
Greater Manchester	Bolton	265	111	5685	6180	9
Gwent	Blaenau Gwent	68	30	1436	1510	5
Hampshire	Basingstoke & Deane	157	64	3213	3460	8
Hertfordshire	Broxbourne	86	35	1532	1404	-8
Humberside	East Riding of Yorkshire	327	138	4112	4628	13
Kent	Ashford	110	44	1548	1499	-3
Lancashire	Blackburn with Darwen	140	55	3306	2973	-10
Leicestershire	Blaby	91	37	985	986	0
Lincolnshire	Boston	58	25	1125	1098	-2
London, City of	City of London	9	5	942	967	3
Merseyside	Knowsley	149	61	3074	1906	-38
Metropolitan Police	Barking & Dagenham	465	67	5288	5150	-3
Norfolk	Breckland	127	53	1440	1351	-6
Northamptonshire	Corby	54	22	1427	1523	7
Northumbria	Alnwick	32	14	249	363	46
North Wales	Conwy	112	50	2119	2513	19
North Yorkshire	Craven	54	23	674	603	-11
Nottinghamshire	Ashfield	114	48	1914	1881	-2
South Wales	Bridgend	131	55	1990	1757	-12
South Yorkshire	Barnsley	222	95	4350	4158	-4
Staffordshire	Cannock Chase	93	38	2169	2443	13
Suffolk	Babergh	85	36	725	724	0
Surrey	Elmbridge	130	53	1216	1554	28
Sussex	Adur	59	26	797	777	-3
Thames Valley	Aylesbury Vale	168	66	2367	2746	16
Warwickshire	North Warwickshire	62	26	588	647	10
West Mercia	Bridgnorth	52	22	407	426	5
West Midlands	Birmingham	1001	399	25,267	26,280	4
West Yorkshire	Bradford	485	186	11,389	9647	-15
Wiltshire	Kennet	77	30	651	836	28

Violence against the person: offences per 1000 population 06/07	Burglary dwelling: offences recorded 05/06	Burglary dwelling: offences recorded 06/07	Burglary dwelling: change 05/06–06/07 (%)	Burglary dwelling: offences per 1000 population 06/07	Burglary dwelling: offences per 1000 households 06/07	Theft of a motor vehicle: offences recorded 05/06	Theft of a motor vehicle: offences recorded 06/07	Theft of a motor vehicle: change 05/06–06/07 (%)	Theft of a motor vehicle: offences per 1000 population 06/07
17	500	673	35	4	9	613	615	0	4
16	924	794	-14	5	13	612	465	-24	3
18	705	942	34	8	20	322	335	4	3
20	596	509	-15	4	10	406	312	-23	3
29	623	636	2	7	17	468	395	-15	4
15	253	192	-24	2	5	267	234	-12	2
16	409	470	15	4	9	308	295	-4	2
11	151	147	-3	2	4	114	90	-21	1
29	838	575	-31	4	8	59	528	4	3
16	182	162	-11	3	7	109	99	-9	2
16	366	314	-14	2	4	273	267	-2	2
14	823	1072	30	6	15	1107	873	-21	5
25	637	785	19	7	15	410	390	-5	3
23	2429	2260	-7	9	20	1417	1267	-11	5
22	234	198	-15	3	7	397	363	-9	5
22	476	611	28	4	10	401	267	-33	2
16	420	410	-2	5	12	423	387	-9	4
14	1079	1165	8	4	8	726	644	-11	2
14	409	328	-20	3	7	245	247	1	2
21	815	676	-17	5	12	413	410	-1	3
11	300	309	3	3	8	195	183	-6	2
19	237	258	9	4	10	130	120	-8	2
105	25	37	48	4	7	74	75	1	8
13	985	805	-18	5	13	1024	771	-25	5
31	1119	1196	7	7	18	1412	1159	-18	7
11	142	148	4	1	3	245	224	-9	2
28	395	282	-29	5	13	402	323	-20	6
11	38	36	-5	1	3	25	40	60	1
23	279	209	-25	2	4	201	157	-22	1
11	139	175	26	3	8	79	67	-15	1
17	874	933	7	8	19	440	486	10	4
13	404	486	20	4	9	620	575	-7	4
19	1323	1107	-15	5	12	1367	1229	-10	6
26	367	427	16	5	11	326	296	-9	3
9	163	121	-26	1	3	114	118	4	1
12	487	517	6	4	10	204	211	3	2
13	179	120	-33	2	5	138	159	15	3
16	681	611	-10	4	9	349	288	-17	2
10	295	286	-3	5	11	236	227	-4	4
8	96	92	-4	2	4	90	88	-2	2
26	8509	7952	-7	8	20	6311	5262	-17	5
20	3597	3942	10	8	21	2557	2334	-9	5
11	205	177	-14	2	6	82	82	0	1

Source: adapted from Home Office, 2008 (the Home Office website from which this data was taken is a useful site for viewing all the most recent data on crime and crime control policy)

Comment

The main value of such statistical data is that it offers a public record – however limited – of the work of public institutions that need to be publicly accountable. Such evidence is surely better than none. This noted, the evidence is also highly selective. Why, for example, include theft from a vehicle rather than hate crime or antisocial behaviour as one of the comparative indicators of successful reduction of crime *and* disorder? Furthermore, it is highly problematic to judge the success or failure of preventive institutions, such as CDRPs and CSPs, from annual reductions in the recorded incidence of crime rates. It is clearly possible to have 'successful' CDRPs and CSPs, when assessed in terms of innovative and targeted initiatives or genuine multi-agency commitment, which may be faced with increases in crime and disorder due to factors beyond their control. These external factors range from demographic changes in the population, and the 'private actions' taken by citizens and businesses with regard to securing their goods and property, to the effects of heightened economic inequalities. It is also evident that crime and disorder reduction strategies may, in the short term at least, lead to increased reporting of previously hidden crimes and result superficially in reductive target failure, as is likely to be the case with initiatives associated with previously hidden or under-reported crimes such as domestic abuse and hate crimes.

However, there are other types of evidence that have been associated with this policy field. Smaller-scale evaluations of specific initiatives and projects – especially those that can be measured in a 'before-and-after' fashion – are the other main source of evidence and proof of success or failure in crime prevention and community safety. Extract 4.1, from the UK Government's Department for Communities and Local Government (DCLG) White Paper *Strong and Prosperous Communities*, is typical of the evidence deployed from local 'what works' exemplars, including statistical backing with regard to crime and disorder reduction.

Extract 4.1

Initiatives from across the country reinforce the value of community participation. From the Slade Green project in Bexley, the Make a Difference work in Ipswich, to the Blackthorn partnership in Northampton, the lesson is clear. By providing simple and regular opportunities to discuss concerns and how these could be tackled, local people become more confident that their local authority and other providers are working to meet their needs.

Making communities central to community safety – Slade Green, Bexley

The Slade Green area of Bexley was a deprived area and suffered from high rates of burglary, car crime, disorder, domestic violence, and race related crime. The Slade Green Community Safety Action Zone (CSAZ) was established to develop an ongoing dialogue between residents and statutory partners. Using a variety of engagement methods, the council and partners were able to focus on the issues that really mattered to local residents. A range of policy responses was implemented to tackle the issues that residents identified. Between September 2001 and June 2003 the CSAZ achieved a turnaround in the estate:

- car crime declined by 29%;

- disorder by 13%;

- vandalism by 20%;

- street crime by 25%; and

- fear of crime also dropped with the proportion of residents not feeling safe after dark dropping from 78% to just 7%.

DCLG, 2006a, p. 29

This extract from the White Paper illustrates clearly the rhetorical power of numbers. However, it is possible to identify some of the limitations of the evidence drawn on in this extract when viewed from a social scientific perspective.

It does not stand up to social scientific standards for assessing the validity of the evidential claims made. For example, there is no information or discussion about the mechanisms by which the project in its specific context may have helped to reduce the stated instances of crime and disorder. We are asked to take these correlations on trust. Again, the actual levers in the wider environment of Bexley, which may have led to the decline of crime in this locality, might have been unrelated to the specific initiative and have their root causes elsewhere (e.g. in changes in labour and housing markets, targeted police disruption or repression of street robbers, individual citizens' actions regarding the safeguarding of their property, etc.). We also have no means of assessing the rigour of the evaluation that produced these conclusions on the project in the first place.

Put briefly, 'evaluation research' focuses on the question of whether or not a particular policy or intervention works. The largest body of evidence associated with evaluation research is, unsurprisingly, linked to initiatives that can be most easily 'counted'. In the field of community safety, situational crime prevention initiatives meet the criteria of being most easily measured in terms of effect (especially when compared with longer-term and more diffuse social or community-based initiatives).

Are there any other sources of evidence about the success of community safety work, as institutionalised in local partnerships, above and beyond the statistical league tables and evaluations of specific initiatives noted above? Our starting point in answering this question must be the recognition that there is limited robust research evidence with regard to the performance and outcomes of these partnerships across the country. The evaluation literature associated with the national inspection and evaluation agency of the Audit Commission (1999) and Home Office (2008)-sponsored research emphasises that CDRPs/CSPs have had a problem of managerial change and lack of 'smart' thinking. It is also assumed that 'successful partnerships' means 'successful crime prevention', although, as noted above, there is, of course, no obvious line of causality regarding the impact on crime. Perversely, the 'best' – as in mature, focused, resourced and well-managed – CDRPs/CSPs consistently have high rates of crime and disorder in the government's league tables due to their location in high-density population, highly unequal urban areas. The problem with this line of reasoning for the student of social sciences is that it tends to *decontextualise* how partnerships work and under what conditions. It is unfortunate that 'what works' has too often been synonymous with what can be easily counted in auditing terms.

Qualitative case study-based research from the social scientific academic community across criminology and social policy has revealed that tensions and conflicts, and political struggles between 'partners', remain alongside the pressure to be seen publicly as 'happy' partners working with 'communities' (see Hughes, 2007). These case studies also reveal that local community safety strategies have remained managed largely by a centrally driven performance management agenda in which cost-effective measures for the realisation of (central government) crime reduction targets are prioritised. And yet CDRPs/CSPs have still not been able to prove their success in performance management terms.

The main evidence from these case studies on community safety work has highlighted the tensions and power relations between partners, the divergent intentions and lack of local accountability. Perhaps CDRPs/CSPs are most accurately seen as duopolies (i.e. institutions characterised by the control of two bodies or subjects) of the local authority and the police, despite the formal rhetoric of broadening 'ownership' among a wider range of 'responsible' partners. However, the most striking

'Achilles heel' of the work in the field of community safety has been the lack of any sustained 'involvement' or 'leadership' from local communities. The evidence from case study research suggests that appeals to 'community' in partnership work on community safety have thus remained largely rhetorical and empty of substance. Despite this conclusion, it is important to recognise that community-based governmental experiments provide an acid test of policy-oriented learning about contemporary crime control and safety promotion. In turn, perhaps the very capacious character of community governance offers different political actors the opportunity for advancing their particular agenda for policy change. As Adam Edwards and Gordon Hughes have argued:

> The elusiveness of what 'community' actually means in relation to crime control, the absence of any clear consensus over what constitutes 'community-based crime control', 'community safety', 'community crime prevention' and 'community policing' etc., is a product not of intellectual vacuity but of the political struggles to define the responsibilities for, and strategies of, crime control.
>
> (Edwards and Hughes, 2002, p. 5)

2.3 Crime and disorder reduction and community safety: Tweedledum and Tweedledee?

The discussion so far has shown that there have been national targets and performance indicators to facilitate the compliance of local agencies to deliver services concerning community safety. However, the question of what purposes, standards and values of community safety is such compliance being directed towards remains uncertain. In the contemporary UK the 'official' national government definition of the primary purpose of the new local governance of crime and safety is that of crime and, increasingly, disorder reduction, as the following statement from the DCLG White Paper affirms:

> We want to put community safety at the heart of the place-shaping role of local authorities – reflecting the high priority that local communities place on these issues. ...
>
> [Footnote] The public say that low-level crime, anti-social behaviour and disrespect are the issues that are of most importance to communities locally.
>
> (DCLG, 2006b, p. 5)

However, there is another response to the insecurity of the citizen that has also characterised the recent history of both central and local government – that of a broader social inclusion-driven model of community safety. The implementation of these arguably different and potentially contradictory policy objectives may be producing an underlying tension in the resulting local practices. The goal of crime and disorder reduction is associated with narrow crime control concerns about the performance and delivery of services that aim to reduce the incidence of crime (including antisocial behaviour that has 'crime-like' consequences). In contrast, the goal of community safety may also incorporate social welfare aspirations to construct a new 'public good' of public safety in response to a range of actual and perceived risks and harms (Hope, 2005; Hughes, 2007). The attainment of such a 'public good' aspires to contribute to the 'quality of life' of citizens and, consequently, is associated with identifying and addressing community needs for safety rather than with a narrower concern with targeted crime reduction. The tension between social welfare and crime control in the field of community safety is particularly marked in the strategies and interventions targeted at 'problem populations' (such as the indigenous peoples of Australia, discussed in Section 4).

Whatever the contradictions at play in this policy field, local community safety partnerships in the UK, the USA and Australia continue to be positioned at the forefront of work associated with the state's commitment to deliver a reduction in crime, the fear of crime and, increasingly, antisocial behaviour in local communities. Alongside this social control agenda, however, the use of the technique of multi-agency partnership may reflect a broader challenge associated with governing today: namely the recognition that decision making has multiple locations, both spatial and sectoral, and is driven by the complex interplay of forces across these. It is hard to argue with the claim that complex challenges, such as tackling crime and disorder, and improving people's sense of safety and security, require input from a variety of institutional sources and, in turn, that people have 'joined-up' problems that do not follow the bureaucratic demarcations of traditional public services. The next section looks in more detail at these partnership and policy implementation processes.

3 Partnerships and 'community governance': managing the unmanageable?

The verdict on multi-agency partnership work in community safety is by no means agreed. According to official government discourses increasingly across the world, the cause of partnership working and community engagement, which underpins community safety, is a benign and rational global social policy 'dream-ticket' promoted by such civic communitarians as Putnam (2000) and global institutions like the World Bank (see Chapters 1, 2 and 6 in this volume; also **Cochrane and Walters, 2008**). On the other hand, critics of community safety view it as another worrying sign of a growing 'totalitarianism' whereby more and more of civil society is embroiled in the extended, penetrative and often criminalising network of social control and politics of security (Bauman, 1999; **Cochrane and Talbot, 2008**; Cohen, 1985).

These two contrasting positions both offer in their varying ways compelling narratives. At the same time, they are perhaps too 'smooth' in terms of the story they tell and may, as a result, downplay the contradictory and unfinished consequences associated with this policy field where the logics of welfare and control coalesce in complex ways. This section discusses the evidence available with regard to community safety and its partnership institutions as concrete expressions of community governance.

Figure 4.2

Creating safer communities? This is an image from the Home Office publication *Cutting Crime – A New Partnership 2008–2011*

3.1 Desperately seeking community in local governance?

In his classic text on the new culture of control at the end of the twentieth century, the criminologist David Garland suggests that greater community involvement is unfolding in the multi-agency, preventive sector: 'This network of partnership arrangements and inter-agency working agreements is designed to foster crime prevention and to enhance community safety, primarily through the cultivation of community involvement and the dissemination of crime prevention ideas and practices' (Garland, 2001, p. 16).

For Les Johnston and Clifford Shearing (2003), two of the most influential theorists and policy advocates of the new community governance, this emphasis is allied even more explicitly to a normative celebration of local, community-based networks. Accordingly, they argue that 'The mobilisation of local knowledge is fundamental to the construction of just and democratic forms of security governance' (Johnston and Shearing, 2003, p. 140). According to such optimistic assessments of the empowering potential of community governance, preventive partnerships are exemplary illustrations, built on relations of trust, interdependence and participation in networks, rather than based on hierarchical command and professional control (see Chapters 1, 2 and 3). However, the extent to which preventive partnerships represent such networked governance is an issue that has to be resolved by empirical investigation. Certainly the current enthusiasm for 'appearing' to govern in, through and by communities is particularly marked in the field of local community safety in both the UK and across other Western countries more generally (Hughes et al., 2002). On the basis of the growing body of research evidence to date, a more accurate assessment of the realities of networked community governance 'on the ground' is that the type of communitarian participation, never mind community leadership, envisaged by Garland and by Johnston and Shearing, remains a lofty and often righteous aspiration that is very rarely realised in practice in the work of partnerships.

Previous chapters have already suggested that in the contemporary world community appears in its multiple guises in the processes of governing. It is represented increasingly as the site of governance, the form of governance and the (intended) effect of governance. Communities are seemingly invested with authority and capacity due to their 'politico-moral' agency (Rose, 1999). They also require the attention, respect and interest of statutory, voluntary and private governmental agencies. Meanwhile, communities are viewed as the essential repositories of values and resources that may be 'activated' – or even 'reactivated' – in the process of governing. And increasingly, these new forms of local governing are represented as 'partnerships' as Cochrane and Newman (Chapter 2, Section 4, in this volume) showed in their discussion of the 'Shoreditch Our Way' case study.

This chapter suggests that the instabilities of community as a site, mode and effect of governance are manifold and represent an ever-present challenge for all institutions, groups and agents involved in mobilising and harnessing such collective energies as community or neighbourhood participation. For example, communities are difficult to find when you need them; it is difficult to decide on who are their 'usable' and 'legitimate' representatives; and when they do 'materialise', they are often plural, multi-vocal and contradictory entities. In turn, communities defined by geographical place are often constructed and fissured by different identities and interests. On the other hand, communities defined by identity are themselves riven with divisions and tensions regarding their seemingly 'essentialised' identities and the role of community 'leaders' in embodying and representing these qualities (see Chapters 1 and 3). It is difficult to form communities and hold them stable for the purposes of governance. Nowhere is this more starkly evident, with all its contradictions, than in the increasingly indistinguishable policy fields of community safety and local crime control in recent decades.

Let us now examine some concrete illustrations of the instabilities associated with the reinvention of community as the site, instrument and effect of contemporary governance in the field of community safety.

3.2 Blame it on the experts?

It is important to note the contradiction that policies designed to tackle social exclusion often imply that 'community' is a category applied to the poor, the marginalised and the 'excluded', but rarely to the more affluent and 'included' majority populations. At the same time, the people who live in high-crime areas have generally not been central to the practical enactment of 'community'-based crime prevention efforts. For example, the generally deprived communities consulted by partnerships across the public policy sector, in programmes such as the New Deal for Communities (NDC) in the late 1990s in the UK, had little say in the establishment of the criteria by which such programmes are monitored. In the case of the NDC, in which 'communities' were involved in the projects from the beginning, Marilyn Taylor notes that the monitoring criteria were preset by external consultants, and she quotes a 'community participant' in one neighbourhood renewal project who argued that 'it is about someone else's agenda. They just want you to tinker with this bit or that bit but you are never actually asked to set the priorities' (quoted in Taylor, 2003, p. 124).

As a consequence, agencies charged with constructing community-based programmes have often largely ignored the core constituency of a community and then determine that it cannot be relied on as an agent of change (see also Chapter 2). In the specific field of community safety 'all too frequently high crime communities are perceived to be full of "problem people", not people who may have problems' (Foster, 2002, p. 168). Crawford has also noted that appeals to community and partnership do not necessarily undermine the expertise of top-down specialist agencies in 'community-based' crime prevention: 'Despite the apparent critique of "expertise" implicit in appeals to "community" and "partnership", the reality remains highly reliant upon expert knowledge which managerialises any significant community input or control. Rather than the end of professional expertise, "partnerships" reconstitute a new model of professionalisation' (Crawford, 1997, p. 224). Karen Evans's research (2004), on local preventive partnerships in England, suggests that often experts have accepted community involvement only on their own terms.

There are, of course, much-lauded exceptions to these processes of marginalisation of community involvement, such as the award-winning Safer Neighbourhood Partnership Scheme in Birmingham in the 2000s. This focused on five deprived and crime-ridden neighbourhoods where it appeared that local people were not just consulted but were involved in 'steering' the projects. What remains uncertain even in this exceptional example is 'which' local people were engaged and empowered and 'which' were perhaps excluded from community involvement.

Much of the critique of attempts to generate community-based preventive work, and to involve communities in this work, points to the problems associated with professional, bureaucratic and managerial interests in the agencies of the state at various levels. This of course runs the risk of both seeing public agencies as the problem and celebrating the 'community' simultaneously as victim and potential saviour. In practice, things are usually more complex. For example, social researchers Michael Shiner et al. (2004) highlight, in their qualitative study of 'community responses to drugs', the complex issues surrounding appeals to community involvement in this highly charged area of policy and practice. They argue that, superficially at least, there is widespread support among the relevant agencies for the principle of community involvement, but at a deeper level there is little agreement as to what this might mean or what form it should take. Many professionals in the drugs field are concerned about the hostility of local communities to the demonised drug user and their seeming wish to exclude and expel drug users *tout court* from their midst. Shiner et al. (2004, p. 10) also discovered that many 'experts', such as drug and alcohol action team (DAAT) coordinators, were acutely aware of the limits to genuine community involvement in the supposed community-based work of governmental agencies, including their own work. To quote one such coordinator:

> A lot of things fall down because of a lack of time and money, it's all about tokenism. We all say we involve the community and then go and do these tokenistic things – public meetings and consultation – but we don't go through a process where we educate the community,

we don't think in terms of long-term investment to make the
community more effective.

(Quoted in Shiner et al., 2004, p. 10)

Such views are perhaps expressive neither of a conspiratorial professional
defensiveness nor of a deliberate wish to 'managerialise' community
input in partnership work. Rather, they show the inherently difficult
and demanding nature of attempting innovative, 'bottom-up' and
socially inclusive community capacity-building work. This work is
particularly difficult when it involves 'problem populations' such as the
drug users in the study by Shiner et al. where there may well be a strong
popular impulse to banish such groups or individuals from the
community.

In the UK many of the most deprived and marginalised communities are
witnessing a displacement of risk on to those least able to bear it (Taylor,
2003, p. 214). In other words, it is often the poorest communities –
'communities of fate' – into which vulnerable people and/or people with
problems either drift or are placed by policymakers. Indicative of such
processes are such examples as the resettlement of previously convicted
paedophiles in the most deprived and marginalised housing estates, and
the forced dispersal and settlement of asylum seekers in inner city areas.

Activity 4.5

Read the following extract from the crime novelist Ian Rankin, which
describes a fictional run-down housing estate in Edinburgh and its latest
inhabitants, newly 'dispersed' asylum seekers as encountered by Rankin's
detective hero, John Rebus. What and who does Rankin graphically
capture here in terms of poverty, policy practices and vulnerable
populations? What might be the consequences of the various conflicting
processes that are being described?

Extract 4.2

Knoxland was not a popular estate. It tended to attract only the
desperate and those with no choice in the matter. In the past, it had
been used as a dumping ground for tenants the council found hard to
house elsewhere, addicts and the unhinged. More recently, immigrants
had been catapulted into its dankest, least welcoming corners. Asylum-
seekers, refugees. People nobody really wanted to think about or have
to deal with.

Rankin, 2004, p. 5

Comment

Although this is a fictional example, it is one that is based on an all too real case of the murder of an asylum seeker in a run-down housing estate in Glasgow, and it speaks to the experiences of other communities – those 'hard places' of often trapped and disadvantaged people – across the world. Such communities may be viewed as victims of top-down initiatives whereby significant numbers of vulnerable people, whether they are ex-offenders, refugees or people with mental health problems, are introduced into already vulnerable areas without either prior consultation or preparation for such settlement schemes. Not surprisingly, the consequences may be a dangerously potent brew of defensive community activism. The consequences of this can be seen in incidents of violence and conflict – for example, the murder of Firsat Yildiz Dag, a Kurdish refugee in Glasgow's Sighthill estate in 2001, and the anti-Iraqi Kurdish refugee riots on the Caia Park estate in Wrexham, North Wales in 2003.

Figure 4.3

Examples of communities protesting: campaigning against Home Office plans (a) to open a hostel for registered paedophiles, and (b) for an asylum seeker centre

While such defensive community mobilisations are highly problematic, nevertheless it is important to take on board the wider social context for, as Taylor observes:

> the more privileged in society lobby more subtly and more successfully to ensure that the most vulnerable or threatening people do not end up in their back yard, or they simply buy their way out of that kind of risk. However, as risk is displaced on to those least able to bear it communities that are already stressed are expected to take on extra pressure, without the resources to do so.
>
> (Taylor, 2003, p. 214)

4 Managing 'problem populations': colonial dreams, indigenous nightmares

The focus in this section is on *what* and *who* is being governed by the new institutional infrastructure and occupational practices referred to earlier. So far this chapter has focused mainly on UK developments in the policy field of community safety and crime prevention. At this point the chapter metaphorically 'shifts gears' and briefly explores the transnational nature of these policy processes by looking at the specific example of policy initiatives regarding the social welfare and crime control agenda in relation to indigenous peoples in contemporary Australia. The fate of indigenous peoples provides a dramatic and often tragic example of the consequences of top-down government initiatives under the banner of community-based crime prevention. Tellingly, these processes from 'elsewhere' in the globe (for UK readers) also illustrate important policy lessons to be learned from comparative scrutiny.

The history of indigenous peoples' experiences at the hands of the public authorities in colonial and postcolonial Australia is a tale of victimisation, 'state crimes' and attempted cultural annihilation. Crucially, however, it is also a story of the survival and struggle of some of the most marginalised and excluded populations, in terms of the dominant culture and laws of any contemporary society globally (see Blagg, 2008a). This specific case is also illustrative of the continued use of 'community' as an identity descriptor and an almost magical policy solution, even though indigenous Australians do not constitute 'community' in the narrow sense of being a geographically and territorially settled entity (see Chapter 1).

Defining indigenous peoples

Adapting the argument of the Inter-American Development Bank, Laura Capobianco has suggested the following criteria for defining indigenous peoples around the world. Indigenous people are:

1 descendants from populations inhabiting a country at the time of conquest or colonisation

2 irrespective of their legal status or current residence, people who retain some or all of their own social, economic, cultural and political institutions and practices

3 people who recognise themselves as belonging to indigenous or pre-colonial cultures.

(Adapted from Capobianco, 2006, p. 3)

Figure 4.4
A rural Aboriginal-Australian camp in Northern Territory; Aboriginal-Australian teenagers in a Sydney suburb; an Aboriginal-Australian designed anti-alcohol poster

The quantitative evidence – including official statistics – coming from both government and independent research across Australia shows that the Aboriginal peoples of Australia continue to be disproportionately represented in categories of vulnerability (e.g. drug and alcohol abuse) and within the criminal justice system. For example, statistically, in the early years of this century Aboriginal people represented 2 per cent of the population of Australia, yet they constituted 20 per cent of all prisoners. In Western Australia (WA) in the same period over 42 per cent of the adult prison population was Aboriginal. Meanwhile, indigenous young people represented 4 per cent of the WA population, yet made up around 80 per cent of all youths in detention. In turn, Aboriginal women in WA were twenty-nine times more likely to be incarcerated than non-Aboriginal women. Rates of victimisation were also disproportionate. The criminologist Harry Blagg (2008a) notes that Aboriginal women were forty-five times more likely to be victims of violence (often alcohol fuelled) than non-Aboriginal women. Such quantitative data confirms the importance of large-scale demographic statistical evidence for social scientific research and analysis in uncovering some of the social facts of life for large collectivities of people over time. It is hard to imagine more compelling evidence than this of the damaging effects of direct government interventions. The dominant response of national governments to the problems 'of' and 'with' indigenous peoples in Australia, historically, has been to see the issues of unemployment, poor education, abuse, alcohol and drug dependency, and criminal behaviours as residing in Aboriginal culture itself, thereby suggesting that 'if only Aboriginal people would stop being Aboriginal we could help them' (Blagg, 2008a, p. 1). As Blagg (2008a) notes, front-line policing remains fixated on managing 'the Aboriginal problem', and arrest and detention are most often viewed as first resort tools of order maintenance.

More broadly across the world, there is official statistical evidence of the over-representation of indigenous people in criminal justice systems, combined with social and economic disadvantage, alongside high rates of suicide, accidents, illness, family violence, sexual abuse, unemployment and low educational achievement relative to the non-indigenous populations. Given this increasingly public recognition of a crisis of legitimacy in traditional national government responses to the problems of indigenous peoples, there is a growing acceptance among both activists and public agencies that the very broad range and nature of the risk factors involved require multifaceted, more inclusive and bottom-up interventions developed by community safety and community governance projects. According to the International Crime Prevention Centre (Capobianco, 2006), bottom-up community capacity-building interventions offer the way forward. Indeed, even the most prominent academic critics of the often fused government crime control and welfare policies regarding Aboriginal peoples in Australia (Blagg, 2008b; Cunneen, 2001) support this broad shift to a focus on self-determination, Aboriginal human rights, recognition of traditional law and customs, and working via holistic, multifaceted rather than narrowly top-down crime prevention and welfare initiatives. Of course, such critics emphasise that there is a danger that this alternative approach may remain purely rhetorical and not affect the actual practices of the state police and welfare agencies.

However, despite these more recent bottom-up, community-focused directions in social welfare and crime control policy, the dominant interventions based on the assumption that the problems reside in Aboriginal culture are still very much in evidence. For example, the continuation of this approach is captured in the statement given in Extract 4.3, made in August 2007 with regard to the National Emergency Response Bill (NERB) from the Australian central government and the then Minister for Families, Community Services and Indigenous Peoples. This statement was made in the light of evidence that showed very high levels of child abuse, violence and substance misuse in some Northern Territory Aboriginal settlements.

Activity 4.6

Read through the statement in Extract 4.3 and make a note of:

- the blaming of problems on Aboriginal culture

- the various examples of the convergence of social welfare concerns and crime control concerns

- the type of national government intervention that is being advocated here.

Extract 4.3

When confronted with a failed society where basic standards of law and order and behaviour have broken down and where women and children are unsafe, how should we respond? ...
Six weeks ago, the *Little Children are Sacred* report commissioned by the Northern Territory Government confirmed what the Government had been saying. It told us in the clearest possible terms that child sexual abuse among Aboriginal children in the Northern Territory is serious, widespread and often unreported, and that there is a strong association between alcohol abuse and sexual abuse of children. With clear evidence that the Northern Territory Government was not

able to protect these children adequately, the Howard Government [i.e. Australia's then national government] decided that it was now time to intervene and declare an emergency situation and use the Territories Power available under the Constitution to make laws for the Northern Territory.

We are providing extra police, we will stem the flow of alcohol, drugs and pornography, assess the health situation of children, engage local people in improving living conditions, and offer more employment opportunities and activities for young people. We aim to limit the amount of cash available for alcohol, drugs and gambling during the emergency period and make a strong link between welfare payments and school attendance.

Australian Government, 2007

Comment

The emphasis at the beginning of this extract, on a 'failed society' without the 'basic standards of law and order', reflects a focus on the ways in which people behave rather than on wider contexts or processes that may affect people's behaviour. Even critics of this much-publicised National Emergency Response Bill and its programme of interventions accepted that there was no denying the self-destructive forces at work in many Aboriginal communities, not least affecting the most vulnerable individuals, such as children, and often associated with family violence by males against females. The different forms of violence cited here provide examples of the convergence between social welfare and crime control concerns, or the link that is established between welfare payments and school attendance or between alcohol abuse and extra police. In responding to this situation, the view of the national government at that time was that a top-down, largely militaristic solution to the crisis of community safety was required. The range of interventions proposed emphasised coercive 'outside' solutions, rather than the facilitation of bottom-up solutions within communities themselves. The consequences of this type of response were shaped by Aboriginal memories and experiences of earlier coercive social welfare policy interventions. As one critic noted:

> It took many back to the horror of the infamous 'stolen generation', thousands of Aboriginal children taken, often forcibly, from their families into institutions in a misguided attempt at assimilation throughout the twentieth century. Despite Howard's [Australia's then Prime Minister] reassurances, fear and panic were reported to have seized Aboriginal communities. Families were already fleeing to the bush, fearful of seeing soldiers take their children away.
>
> (Flanagan, 2007, p. 35)

The reference to the 'stolen generation' here concerns the Australian government policy, from the 1880s to as recently as the late 1960s, to remove indigenous children forcibly from their parents due to perceived inadequate standards of upbringing, and to place them with childless white Australian couples or in children's institutions in order to 'Westernise' and 'civilise' them. Many of these children were never able to make contact again with their parents and communities. The levels of institutionalised abuse that followed this enforced removal have slowly emerged from the previously silenced voices of the survivors of this coercive and inhumane policy – a policy predicated on racist assumptions of moral superiority of the white settlers of Australia.

Figure 4.5
The poster for the 2002 film *Rabbit-Proof Fence*. The film told the story of the long homeward journey made by three mixed heritage Aboriginal girls who had been forcibly removed from their families under the then Australian government's race policy of placing Aboriginal children in state 'care'

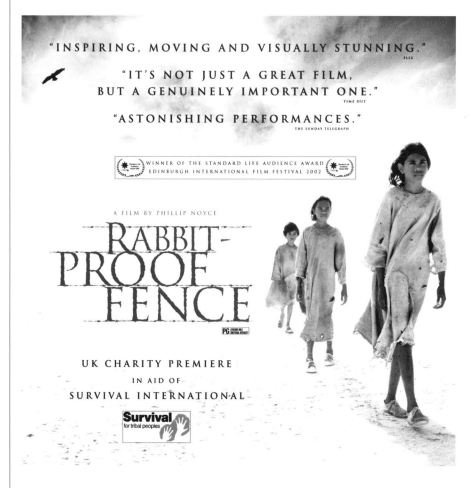

Critics of NERB, such as Blagg (2008b), have argued that if the Bill became law many of the community-based reforms developed since the 1990s would unravel in the face of the new coercive paternalism designed to break down what remains of the distinct Aboriginal 'domain' (i.e. a domain made up of separate traditions, law, kinship ties, religion, etc.). However, the Bill provoked a widespread backlash which, in part, led to the defeat of Howard's Liberal Party in the 2007 Australian election:

> Howard's response – a five year takeover of 60 indigenous communities with soldiers and police overseeing alcohol and pornography bans, the part quarantining of welfare payments to ensure money is spent on food and other necessities, and the compulsory testing of Aboriginal children for sexual abuse – stunned Australia. Initial confusion soon gave way to condemnation of the plan as draconian, racist, unworkable, an ill-conceived shock-and-awe campaign.
>
> (Flanagan, 2007, p. 35)

This example of the National Emergency Response Bill illustrates the potential for community safety interventions to take extreme authoritarian and damaging forms, which not only create fear and tension but also strengthen the association of Aboriginal communities with criminal behaviours. At the same time, that there was a hostile reaction to the Bill among the Australian electorate, and that the Bill was defeated in the Australian parliament is also indicative of other more progressive discourses for promoting safer communities (Blagg, 2008a, p. 95). The defeat of NERB appears to imply the growing policy and political dominance – in this particular context – of the community safety governance model. For it has been argued by leading researchers and policy advisers, such as Blagg (2008a), that successful initiatives – in terms of harm reduction among Aboriginal people – are more likely to be found in such bottom-up and partnership initiatives as Aboriginal Community Patrols and Night Patrols. According to one commentator:

> the object of the patrol is not to assist in removing intoxicated persons from the streets. This is a frequent cause of misunderstanding for the police and the general public. The object is to resolve problems in the town camps and special purpose leases; to settle disputes when they begin and not after they have exploded, drawing in extended families or entire tribal groups.
>
> (Curtis, 1992, cited in Blagg, 2008a, p. 128)

Blagg (2008a, p. 132) notes that such patrols, which also have a high level of involvement of Aboriginal women, 'reflect the extent to which the Aboriginal community still exists at some distance from non-Indigenous government structures and, to a large extent, from non-Indigenous civil society'. Such initiatives appear able to provide both a link and a 'buffer' between Aboriginal communities and government agencies. Other successes include family violence offender programmes, which remain Aboriginal community 'owned' (and not just 'based') and linked to Aboriginal customary law while nonetheless having strong links with relevant agencies and courts (Blagg, 2008a).

In summary, the key arguments of Section 4 are as follows. First, the section began with a broad outline of the Australian context and how Aboriginal people have been both represented and, in turn, governed by the state authorities on the basis of being a danger and a problem, but also as populations who are vulnerable and have compounded social problems. Second, the section examined how the responses to the perceived problems associated with indigenous communities tend to generate unstable mixtures of the historically dominant, top-down, draconian, direct government interventions alongside, more recently, inclusive and bottom-up community safety and community governance-inspired interventions. Third, it was argued that these responses are often in conflict, and a recent example of this collision was given, namely the National Emergency Response Bill and the reactions to this proposed legislation. In discussing this, it was argued that the Bill and the public reaction to it exemplify more generally the hybrid character of such processes of managing problem populations, involving both welfare and crime control logics. In comparative terms, the discussion of this Australian/Aboriginal case shows the ability of community safety to work in very diverse and transnational settings.

5 Review

This chapter has examined how the contemporary policy field of community safety may be said to exemplify both the entanglements between social welfare and crime control policies and their contradictory tendencies. The chapter has argued that because community safety interventions can be understood as an example of the convergence of these two worlds, it represents a *hybrid* policy field. The emergence and implementation of community safety approaches were examined in two geographical contexts, namely the community safety and crime reduction programme in the UK and the attempts at governing the crime and welfare problems of indigenous peoples in contemporary Australia. In plotting the comparative developments in this relatively new policy field of community safety, the chapter has:

■ Highlighted the ways in which 'problem populations' – that is, those groups of people who are viewed as both vulnerable and dangerous – are sources of concern for social welfare and crime control policy due to their perceived inadequate qualities as an imagined 'good' community.

■ Explored the policy shifts towards the managing of 'problem populations' through the concept of community rather than through 'outside', direct government interventions. The chapter has shown how this shift can involve a tense, uneasy and often contradictory mix of partnership working between different public agencies. Alongside this, it has suggested that securing the involvement of local communities themselves, and especially the excluded and/or difficult members of those local communities, presents a series of continual challenges.

■ Examined the relationship between evidence and policy and shown in particular how stress has been placed, by policymakers in the UK context, on the need for evidence to show 'what works' in relation to community safety initiatives. The dominance of 'what works' in relation to evidence and policymaking reflects the acutely political context of crime control policy approaches. The chapter has looked at how the 'what works' data collection does have a quantitative bias, although the concern of the 'what works' approach with this question means that the evaluation of smaller-scale policy initiatives and local approaches has also become a focus of evidence collection and policy development interest.

The chapter has argued that social welfare and crime control policies seek not only to manage 'problem populations' in order to protect other 'normal' members of communities and their safety, but also, where possible, to normalise these 'problem populations' and the seemingly antisocial and thus 'anti-community' behaviour that defines them.

Further reading

Harry Blagg's *Crime, Aboriginality and the Decolonisation of Justice* (2008, Willan) provides a forceful account and analysis of the complex issues surrounding the past, present and future relations between indigenous, Aboriginal culture and that of the Australian state with regard to crime, justice and community safety. It is also a telling critique of modern, Western assumptions about the nature of the problems associated with indigenous populations. *The Politics of Crime and Community* by Gordon Hughes (2007, Palgrave Macmillan) offers a comprehensive overview of comparative developments in the new governance of community safety and local crime and disorder control. The book provides the reader with an authoritative yet accessible overview of this increasingly salient policy field, in which crime control policy meets social policy, and offers several case studies of some of the most pressing issues associated with this new culture of community control, including antisocial behaviour and the 'youth problem', asylum seeking, migration and community cohesion.

References

Audit Commission (1999) *Safety in Numbers: Promoting Community Safety*, London, Audit Commission.

Australian Government (2007) *Speeches: Northern Territory National Emergency Response Bill 2007: Second Reading Speech* [online], http://www.facs.gov.au/internet/minister3.nsf/content/nter_bill_7aug07.htm (Accessed 11 July 2008).

Bauman, Z. (1999) *In Search of Politics*, Cambridge, Polity Press.

Blagg, H. (2008a) *Crime, Aboriginality and the Decolonisation of Justice*, Cullompton, Willan.

Blagg, H. (2008b) 'Colonial critique and critical criminology' in Cunneen, C. and Anthony, T. (eds) *Essays in Critical Criminology*, Sydney, Federation Press.

Capobianco, L. (2006) *Community Safety Partnerships by and with Indigenous People*, Montreal, International Crime Prevention Centre.

Cochrane, A. and Talbot, D. (eds) (2008) *Security: Welfare, Crime and Society*, Maidenhead, Open University Press/Milton Keynes, The Open University.

Cochrane, A. and Walters, R. (2008) 'The globalisation of social justice' in Newman and Yeates (eds) (2008).

Cohen, S. (1985) *Visions of Social Control*, Cambridge, Polity Press.

Cook, D. (2006) *Criminal and Social Justice*, London, Sage.

Crawford, A. (1997) *The Governance of Crime*, Oxford, Clarendon.

Crawford, A. (1998) *Crime Prevention and Community Safety: Politics, Policies and Practices*, Harlow, Longman.

Crawford, A. (2007) 'Crime prevention and community safety' in Maguire, M., Morgan, R. and Reiner, R. (eds) *Oxford Handbook of Criminology* (4th edn), Oxford, Oxford University Press.

Cunneen, C. (2001) *The Impact of Crime Prevention on Aboriginal Communities*, Sydney, New South Wales Crime Prevention Division and Aboriginal Justice Advisory Council.

Department for Communities and Local Government (DCLG) (2006a) *Strong and Prosperous Communities* (Vol. I), London, Department for Communities and Local Government; also available online at http://www.communities.gov.uk/documents/localgovernment/pdf/152456.pdf (Accessed 10 May 2008).

Department for Communities and Local Government (DCLG) (2006b) *Strong and Prosperous Communities* (Vol. II), London, Department for Communities and Local Government; also available online at http://www.communities.gov.uk/documents/localgovernment/pdf/154067.pdf (Accessed 10 May 2008).

Edwards, A. and Hughes, G. (2002) 'Introduction' in Hughes and Edwards (eds) (2002).

Edwards, A. and Hughes, G. (2008a) *The Role of the Community Safety Officer in Wales: Challenges and Opportunities*, Cardiff, Cardiff School of Social Sciences Working Papers.

Edwards, A. and Hughes, G. (2008b) 'Resilient Fabians: anti-social behaviour and community safety work in Wales' in Squires, P. (ed.) *ASBO Nation*, Bristol, The Policy Press.

Evans, K. (2004) 'Crime control partnerships: who do we trust?', *Criminal Justice Matters*, no. 50, pp. 12–13.

Flanagan, R. (2007) 'This draconian outrage has shaken Australia awake', *The Guardian*, 28 June, p. 3.

Foster, J. (2002) 'People pieces' in Hughes and Edwards (eds) (2002).

Garland, D. (2001) *The Culture of Control*, Oxford, Oxford University Press.

Home Office (2008) *Crime in England and Wales 2006/2007* [online], http://www.homeoffice.gov.uk/rds/crimeew0607.html (Accessed 3 February 2008).

Hope, T. (2005) 'The new local governance of community safety in England and Wales', *Canadian Journal of Criminology and Criminal Justice*, vol. 47, no. 2, pp. 369–88.

Hughes, G. (1998) *Understanding Crime Prevention: Social Control, Risk and Modernity*, Buckingham, Open University Press.

Hughes, G. (2006) 'Community safety' in McLaughlin, E. and Muncie, J. (eds) *The Sage Dictionary of Criminology* (2nd edn), London, Sage.

Hughes, G. (2007) *The Politics of Crime and Community*, Basingstoke, Palgrave Macmillan.

Hughes, G. and Edwards, A. (eds) (2002) *Crime Control and Community: The New Politics of Public Safety*, Cullompton, Willan.

Hughes, G. and McLaughlin, E. (2002) 'Together we'll crack it: partnership and the governance of crime prevention' in Glendinning, C., Powell, D. and Rummery, K. (eds) *Partnership, New Labour and the Governance of Welfare*, Bristol, The Policy Press.

Hughes, G., McLaughlin, E. and Muncie, H. (eds) (2002) *Crime Prevention and Community Safety: New Directions*, London, Sage.

Johnston, L. and Shearing, C. (2003) *Governing Security: Explorations in Policing and Justice*, London, Routledge.

Mooney, G. (2008) '"Problem" populations, "problem" places' in Newman and Yeates (eds) (2008).

Newman, J. and Yeates, N. (eds) (2008) *Social Justice: Welfare, Crime and Society*, Maidenhead, Open University Press/Milton Keynes, The Open University.

Putnam, R.D. (2000) *Bowling Alone: The Collapse and Revival of American Community*, New York, Simon & Schuster.

Rankin, I. (2004) *Fleshmarket Close*, London, Orion.

Rose, N. (1999) *Powers of Freedom: Reframing Political Thought*, Cambridge, Cambridge University Press.

Shiner, M., Thom, B. and MacGregor S. (2004) *Exploring Community Responses to Drugs*, York, Joseph Rowntree Foundation.

Taylor, M. (2003) *Public Policy in the Community*, Basingstoke, Palgrave Macmillan.

Chapter 5
Communities and social mobilisations

Sharon Pinkney and Esther Saraga

Contents

1   Introduction

At the centre of this book is an emphasis on the very different ways in which the concept of community is understood. In the previous chapters you have read discussions of communities as inclusionary sites of belonging, attachment and social order; as exclusionary sites of conflict, boundary and disorder; as sites in which 'problem populations' and places are identified; as sites of social well-being and trust; and as the focus of social policy interventions. It is clear from these discussions that 'community' is both contested and contradictory. In this chapter we, too, will examine ways in which community rejects any single or settled meaning. The chapter will develop the argument that community is an 'unruly' concept as it considers the ways in which people *enact* community. By this we mean that we are interested in the ways in which people use the idea of, or their sense of, community as a basis for practices and actions. These practices and actions vary – they may be mundane and everyday, or they may arise from specific sets of concerns, events or situations.

Activity 5.1

It would be helpful to think about what we mean by enacting community by starting with your own experiences:

■ What kinds of communities do you feel that you belong to, and what helps you to belong? Are there also communities from which you feel excluded?

■ In what ways do you, or people you know, get together to act as a community? What happens in your street, estate, neighbourhood or village that brings people together? Are some of these collective actions based on common identities rather than place?

■ Try to think of activities connected with daily life as well as those that might be seen as social or political campaigns.

Comment

■ Your feelings of belonging or not belonging may stem from many different sources: from bumping into neighbours in the street; meeting people at the shops, in a café or pub or in the park; having an allotment; or walking your dog. They may derive from shared membership of groups or organisations. Meeting other parents at the school gates or sharing childcare can help parents feel part of a community; at the same time, not being involved in many local services and facilities can lead to feelings of exclusion or marginalisation. If you live in an ethnically diverse area, you may have a sense of some spaces or facilities associated with particular ethnic groups, and of other places or spaces where people interact across this diversity.

■ When considering forms of community activity you may have been involved in, your list might be quite long and quite diverse. Below are a range of activities that we thought of:

(a) informal social or educational: reading groups; dog training classes; local choirs; street parties

(b) informal self-help: neighbours supporting older people at home; local parents sharing childcare, setting up playgroups or an after school scheme

(c) organised collective activities around security and crime control: Neighbourhood Watch schemes; campaigns against prostitutes working in local streets

(d) campaigns to save or create services and facilities: a local hospital or swimming pool threatened with closure; for safer road crossings, or improved housing

(e) protests against local developments: a hostel for asylum seekers; housing a known paedophile in the area; motorway and major road construction; a new supermarket or building on green belt and parkland

(f) activities of solidarity supporting people in other countries: collections for natural disasters; global campaigns such as 'Make Poverty History'.

Such a long and diverse list raises questions as to what these very different activities hold in common. Reflecting this focus, the chapter is organised into three main sections. Section 2 looks at the mundane and everyday practices of community and considers the extent to which the social and caring interactions between people can be defined as informal, small-scale acts of welfare. Section 3 then goes on to explore how more organised, semi-formal and formal community-based activity influences policymaking and is able to define and change social and crime control policy agendas. This section argues that community-based campaigns, lobbying and protest can also have an uneasy (and often a conflictual) relation with policymakers. This leads into the final key area of consideration: that community activity may directly challenge existing policy frameworks. Section 4 uses urban unrest and 'disorder' as a case study through which to explore this and to consider how community activity can capture the convergences between the domains of social welfare and crime control.

Figure 5.1

Enacting community: demonstration in support of Burma protestors, London, October 2007; protests by residents and politicians at the proposed site of a hostel for asylum seekers, Worcestershire, 2002; 'Older People's Play Area' in Manchester in 2008 – equipment designed for older people to take exercise

In this context, the aims of the chapter are to:

■ consider how community gets enacted by populations

■ examine the relationship between 'bottom-up' community mobilisations and governing through community

■ consider the ways in which community mobilisations shed further light on the complex connections between social welfare and crime control policies.

2 Small acts: the microworld of community

In this section we start by suggesting that small acts of kindness or neighbourliness – social interactions, conversations and communication, looking after a neighbour's children, feeding pets or keeping an eye on property while neighbours are away, cooking for neighbours who are ill, or baking for a school or local fete, checking on or helping an older person with their shopping – represent everyday social exchanges and supportive behaviours through which people build a local sense of community. We can understand these small acts of social care and social responsibility as being very much part of *informal* welfare and support networks. We can characterise such networks as part of a 'microworld' of community that develops out of these kinds of informal and spontaneous everyday interactions. Reading this will remind you of the discussions of social capital in Chapter 1. Although these mundane practices of kindness and care may be small scale, informal and uneven – not everyone experiences them – they can be understood and experienced as 'features of social life that facilitate coordination and cooperation for mutual benefit' (Putnam, 2003, cited in Moseley and Pahl, 2007, p. 7) and as such are of interest to social researchers and policymakers. As Malcolm Moseley and Ray Pahl (2007, p. 7) note, social capital has been defined in three key ways and these will useful for you to bear in mind as you read this chapter. These are:

■ Bonding social capital: This refers to practices that operate to form a sort of internal 'social glue' between homogeneous (the same) groups within a community.

■ Bridging social capital: This refers to the practices that work outwards to cohere or bridge heterogeneous (different) groups within a community.

■ Linking social capital: This refers to the practices that create connections or make links from a community to external sources of power, outside agencies and resources.

The interest in the possibilities of social capital to deliver social welfare is reflected in the extent to which it is the object of social research. For example, a large-scale quantitative study was conducted by the Health Development Agency (HDA) as part of the General Household Survey 2000/01 in Great Britain into these small acts of community building. The HDA believed that an individual's health and well-being is shaped and constrained by their relationships to social and community networks, and that 'social capital could play a useful role in helping us to understand the extent to which community level relationships and networks might impact on health in local communities' (Coulthard et al., 2002, p. 10). The investigators in the HDA conducted 7857 interviews with randomly selected individuals aged 16 or over in each of the 8221 households in the larger General Household Survey. They used a questionnaire – a series of closed multiple-choice questions – to ask people about the nature of their civic engagement, their relationships with neighbours, their social networks and social support, and their perception of their local area. All these were seen as indicators of social capital. Table 5.1 shows two typical questions on neighbourliness.

Table 5.1 Typical questions

36. Trust
Would you say that you trust ...
most of the people in your neighbourhood ....
many of the people in your neighbourhood ....
a few of the people in your neighbourhood ....
or that you do not trust people in your neighbourhood? ....

44. Speak to neighbours
Not counting the people you live with, how often do you speak to neighbours?
Every day ....
5 or 6 days a week ....
3 or 4 days a week ....
once or twice a week ....
once or twice a month ....
once every couple of months ....
once or twice a year ....
not at all in last 12 months ....

Source: adapted from Coulthard et al., 2002, Appendix B

Let us look at a few of their findings on neighbourliness, social networks and social support.

Neighbourliness

■ 58 per cent of respondents felt they could trust most or many of the people in their neighbourhood.

■ 27 per cent of respondents spoke to neighbours every day; 19 per cent spoke to them less than once a week.

■ 73 per cent of respondents believed that neighbours in their area looked out for each other.

Social networks

■ 30 per cent of respondents had at least five close friends living nearby; 16 per cent had at least five close relatives nearby; 27 per cent had no close friends living in their local area; 44 per cent had no relatives they felt close to living nearby.

■ 66 per cent of respondents had a 'satisfactory friendship network' (they saw or spoke to friends at least once a week and had at least one close friend who lived nearby).

■ 52 per cent of respondents had a 'satisfactory relatives network' (based on similar criteria for relatives).

■ 20 per cent of respondents had neither a network of friends nor of relatives.

Social support

■ 58 per cent of respondents had at least five people they could turn to in a serious personal crisis; 18 per cent had less than three people they could turn to.

■ 90 per cent of respondents had at least one person they could turn to living nearby compared with only 2 per cent of respondents who felt they had nobody to turn to locally.

(Adapted from Coulthard et al., 2002)

The size of the sample allowed the researchers to look at differences in relation to age, region, housing accommodation, household and gender. They found, for example, that there was less neighbourliness among young people (aged 16–24) and people without dependent children. London was also a much less neighbourly area in comparison with the north-east, north-west and south-west of England, which were the most neighbourly. Women had better social networks (in terms of people to speak to on the phone), but men were more likely to have a large number of close friends living nearby. People living in social sector housing, lone parents and single-person households had less social support than those in owner-occupied accommodation, or couples (Coulthard et al., 2002). The findings in the HDA study are mixed – clearly, overall, respondents did have experience of the small acts of community making and social support. However, we do not want to suggest that this is an inevitable or constant experience of community.

The HDA study used a multiple-choice survey to produce statistics that were turned into a measure of social capital, which in turn could be used to draw general conclusions about the relationship between community and well-being.

A very different study, which nevertheless examined very similar questions about the microworld of community and social capital, was conducted by social researchers Anne Power and Helen Willmot (2007) in two low-income neighbourhoods in Leeds and Sheffield in northern England, and two low-income neighbourhoods in east London. The study was conducted over an eight-year period tracking 200 families, and sought to examine how the conditions of an area impacted on the formation or depletion of social capital. Power and Willmot found that their respondents talked extensively about community, social networks, family relations and support within all four areas. The vast majority of respondents felt that they had people to count on and to turn to, and most commonly these were family, friends and/or neighbours. Family contact and support were common among respondents, especially in the Leeds area and especially around childcare and support. Most friends were locally based and 60 per cent of respondents had at least weekly contact with their friends, who were a source of practical and emotional support. The majority of respondents' accounts revealed a high level of trust in their relationships with their neighbours. These accounts highlighted the prevalence of favours – some long-standing and ongoing, and some one-off crisis favours – between neighbours. The study found a high level of participation (around 85 per cent) in entertaining and 'fun' community events.

The HDA study and that by Power and Willmot are both concerned with small aspects of well-being in daily life. Recalling the categorisations of social capital given earlier in this section, we can see evidence not only of bonding but also of bridging social capital. Increasingly, these informal social interactions are seen by policymakers and politicians as crucial for social stability and social cohesion.

3 Organised acts: community activity and its influences on policymaking

In the previous section we focused on the small-scale and everyday ways in which people enact community, and the informal welfare and support networks that these practices give rise to. We noted that in the Power and Willmot study the authors found a high level of participation by their respondents in convivial community events, which provided respondents with a sense of community togetherness and unity. Power and Willmot's findings showed that participation went beyond once-a-year type of involvement in fun community events. Participants in their study would often be active in a range of local social welfare and crime control-related activities. For example, they comment that:

> Across ... the neighbourhoods, respondents were involved with, and in some cases had set up, local groups and initiatives that helped the community and provided links to wider networks.

> Involvement in short term local campaign groups provided some respondents with a chance to 'make a difference'. Participation in ongoing informal neighbourhood crime tackling initiatives actively reduced crime, and respondents' work setting up mother and baby groups filled a gap in the provision of local family services.
>
> (Power and Willmot, 2007, p. 3)

In this part of the chapter we examine some of the more organised forms of community activity for three key reasons – first, to understand how people enacting community can deliver more organised forms of welfare and care; second, to suggest that bottom-up – that is, 'from below' or 'grass-roots' level – activity can highlight issues; and third, because such activity can influence and interact with policymakers and practitioners (see Chapter 2).

Activity 5.2

Read through the short examples of community activity given below and make notes on the following questions:

- How is the community being defined or imagined?

- What kind of community activity or mobilisation is involved?

- What is the relationship between this mobilisation and social policy?

- Can you see instances of linking social capital?

1   The Bogside and Brandywell Women's Group: This group emerged in the Bogside and Brandywell area of Derry in Northern Ireland. These were areas of the city with significant levels of poverty, unemployment, deprivation and political conflict. The gendered experience of the absence of local social amenities and childcare facilities, and the prevalence of marriage breakdown, teenage pregnancies, lone-parent families, domestic violence and social isolation led to a local recognition of the extent of these combined and shared problems. The result was the formation of the Bogside and Brandywell Women's Group in 1994 and its work in creating locally based projects to support women and children (adapted from Bogside and Brandywell Women's Group, undated).

2   Community kitchens in Latin America: These emerged in the impoverished and politically active urban communities across Latin America in the 1970s. For example, in Chile there are over 10,000 community kitchens, or *ollas commun* (common pot). Community kitchens were a response to a chronic lack of basic resources and amenities, and a desire to pool those few that did exist in order to create a sense of solidarity and sociality (Fisher, 1993).

3   South Side Against Closure: This was an umbrella grouping that organised a campaign to save the Govanhill Swimming Pool in Glasgow in 2001. It was a multi-ethnic, multi-age organisation and included a range of local user groups as well as political groupings from across the centre and left of the Scottish political spectrum. The campaign to save the pool was initiated by parents' groups and other pool users' groups. This was an issue that mobilised considerable support from throughout the Govanhill area and the wider city (adapted from Mooney and Fyfe, 2006, p. 137).

4   Community gardens in the Lower East Side, New York: In the 1960s a series of gardens were created out of abandoned brownfield sites by and for local people living in the tenement area of the city. The Lower East Side has been the site of diverse immigration settlements in New York's history and has strong associations with political and community activity. Regentrification processes in New York in the 1980s and 1990s meant that some of the gardens were sold off to developers in the face of local community opposition, and new incoming residents raised concerns about safety and crime in the areas around both the gardens and Tomkins Square Park where homeless people would gather. Some gardens still remain and can be visited. These community gardens represent not only community efforts to create nature spaces, but also migratory histories and identities: some gardens had small buildings made in the

architectural style of countries of departure – for example, Puerto Rican *Casitas* – and some gardens reproduced English cottage garden styles (adapted from Cresswell, 2004, pp. 3–5).

5   In 2004, local Shetland Islanders organised to campaign to stop the deportation of failed asylum seekers who were living on the Islands: 'Furious islanders tell Home Office: "We won't let you take these families from our community"... Here in Shetland a campaign is gathering pace to keep the families in the islands, by means of direct action if necessary. ... Willie Ross, a campaign organiser, said they were not having to work very hard to generate support for both families. ... "There's a lot of us involved who certainly won't let them forcibly remove Tanya and Magnie or Hazel and the two boys without making a noise about it"' (Crawford, 2004).

6   Neighbourhood Watch schemes: These emerged from the concerns of local people about crime and safety. Since the early 1980s they have become widespread across the UK. As described on the Home Office website, Neighbourhood Watch 'is a partnership where people come together to make their communities safer. It involves the Police, Community Safety departments of local authorities, other voluntary organisations and, above all, individuals and families who want to make their neighbourhoods better places to live. It aims to help people protect themselves and their properties and to reduce the fear of crime by means of improved home security, greater vigilance, accurate reporting of suspicious incidents to the police and by fostering a community spirit' (Home Office, 2008).

Comment

In contrast to our earlier discussion, these examples illustrate ways in which communities mobilise in a more organised way around a wide range of issues: to provide or save local services or amenities; to pool resources and address poverty; to create shared spaces; to support disadvantaged women; to lobby for vulnerable groups from other countries; and to protect spaces perceived as unsafe. In all cases there is a sense of shared concerns, grievances or identity, and a collective response made to address these. Taken together, these examples raise questions about the extent to which living in a particular locality makes people into a community. Even though activities may happen within a local area, it is not always place as such that gives people their common interest. Indeed, Deborah Martin (2003) argues that a shared identity in relation to place may have to be imagined in order to mobilise.

Let us consider these examples further. In most of them, place-based identities are complicated by questions of who belongs, or by other identities. In Bogside and Brandywell in Derry, Northern Ireland, it was women in the community who organised around common interests and concerns, developing their own welfare services. Although not run solely by local women, community kitchens are activities in which Latin American women have been particularly participative. The community kitchens can be viewed as part of the resourcefulness in the most impoverished urban areas, which has influenced the social capital-centred policy initiatives increasingly favoured by international organisations such as the World Bank (**Newman and Yeates, 2008**; Chapter 2 in this volume).

Figure 5.2

A soup kitchen in Lima, Peru, serves lunch to poor families, 2002

The anti-deportation community campaign in the Shetland Islands, the Govanhill Swimming Pool campaign and the community gardens in New York can all be understood as forms of organisation that not only are based on local social bonds, but also incorporate more globally inflected identities. You will remember that the community gardens in the Lower East Side were attempts to recreate notions and reminders of home – for example, the little Puerto Rican *Casitas* – in a new country (see the discussion of diasporic identities and community in Chapter 1). The Govanhill campaign involved multicultural and ethnically diverse groups of people acting together to try to save a local amenity (an issue we return to in more detail in Section 3.1). The Shetlands campaign can be understood as being about local attachment to particular individuals, but it also represents a concern with national and international policy on refugees and asylum seekers. Its goal is the inclusion of 'outsiders'. This campaign is part of a large UK and international network of successful campaigns called 'Schools Against Deportation' (2005).

Our earlier discussion in Section 2, on the microworld of community, can help us to understand the wide support for such campaigns: schools are often places of informal social interactions that can foster social bonds across different ethnic communities.

However, as Marilyn Taylor (2003) cautions, it is important not to over-romanticise community actions or the commonality of local concerns. We saw, for instance, in the example of the Lower East Side gardens, that there were tensions between New York City regeneration policy, property developers, long-term residents' attachment to the gardens, and concerns of new residents about crime and safety in the area. Such tensions can be particularly acute in relation to difference and diversity. We saw in Chapter 4 how community activity can be organised in hostile, violent and protectionist ways. The mobilisations in Shetland can be contrasted with attempts in other areas to exclude rather than include asylum seekers. In the UK in 2000, the New Labour Government's proposals to build asylum seeker detention centres in rural and semi-rural areas gave rise to some of the most vociferous and well-organised local anti-asylum campaigns (e.g. in Nottinghamshire and Worcestershire). This community-organised opposition was to be successful as this policy was abandoned (Neal and Agyeman, 2006). Similarly, in South Yorkshire in 2000, local residents objected to plans for an asylum seeker hostel in a private residential area because 'there would be an increase in crime, including vandalism and "social disorder", and that property prices would fall' (Humphries, 2000). Concerns about crime and safety are, of course, key drivers in Neighbourhood Watch schemes. Of all our vignettes it is Neighbourhood Watch that most explicitly represents the direct relationship and integration of community activity with partnership organisations – in this case with the police and local authorities (see Chapter 4). Below, we consider the ways in which community activity works with and makes links to other policymaking and practitioner agencies.

3.1 'Bottom-up' acts and community mobilisations, participation and the policy system

We have suggested that these mobilisations demonstrate the capacity of communities to act autonomously – independently of, or even in opposition to, policy. In the context of community-based policy making, Chapter 2 also looked at the emphasis placed by policymakers on communities having high social capital and being able to act for themselves. So, we can ask to what extent the kinds of 'bottom-up' mobilisations discussed in this chapter are seen by politicians and policymakers as examples of empowered, active communities with high social capital that should be encouraged. It could be argued that such community mobilisations build on and strengthen existing social capital. This has certainly been a key interpretation by policymakers and deliverers, as you have seen in Chapters 2 and 4. The partnership with other agencies and participation of people within their communities has been a specific policy aim and strategy both in the UK and more transnationally.

In the UK, what has become known as the Third Sector is an obvious example of this aim. The Third Sector can be understood as the layer that exists between the types of community activity we have been examining and government agencies. In this layer are grouped community organisations, voluntary organisations, social enterprises and charities. The Third Sector is non-government based and community organisations are central to it. In recognition of the growing importance of non-government social welfare delivery, the UK Government created, rather ironically, an Office of the Third Sector in 2006. This represents the policy emphasis on the need to move to the local, and to deliver policy at and through community, which you have seen in previous chapters in this book. For us, the emergence of the Third Sector category raises broader questions concerning the extent to which community organisations position themselves in relation to formal policy systems. As Taylor notes, this has been a long-standing debate for grass-roots or bottom-up community mobilisations. She argues that 'there are always difficult decisions to be made by communities about whether to be insiders or outsiders in the policy process ... some communities prefer to work outside the system or at least approach government on their own terms rather than allowing themselves to be absorbed into government agendas' (Taylor, 2003, pp. 175–6). However, Taylor goes on to note that there are concrete gains to be made from partnership working and she advocates a balance between being outside enough to remain critical and inside enough to engage with policy agencies and influence decision making. We shall explore these questions further by looking in a bit more detail at one of our earlier case studies – the Save Our Pool/South Side Against Closure campaign in Govanhill.

In order to find out more about the campaign, Gerry Mooney and Nick Fyfe (2006) conducted semi-structured interviews with twelve of the main activists involved (men and women from a diverse range of age, ethnic and occupational backgrounds) during the campaign and immediately after it came to an end. The campaigners were asked about the background to the campaign, why they became involved and how they saw it changing, challenging or reinforcing 'a sense of community' in Govanhill itself.

Activity 5.3

Read the following extract taken from Mooney and Fyfe's findings. Why did this community mobilisation become problematised by the local formal policy system rather than incorporated into it? How is this 'active community' different from the ones discussed in Chapter 2?

Extract 5.1

Govanhill pool was built in 1914 and ... was equipped with a large pool, a smaller pool and a teaching pool, frequently used by four different 'special needs' schools. In addition it also provided much needed private washing and laundry facilities in an area where around 800 houses lacked bathing and washing facilities (these particular services were withdrawn in the 1990s).

While it is easy to romanticise about these buildings, we should also understand the role that they played in the daily fabric of working class life in tenemental Glasgow.

...

However, Govanhill pool also occupied a unique position, catering as it did for the different ethnic groups in the Govanhill area. The existence of three separate pools meant that different groups in the community could make use of the pool. Containing the only secluded pool in Glasgow, the smaller of the main pools was heavily used by women from the local Muslim community whose faith prevents them bathing where they can be seen by men.

...

Within days of the announcement of the closure, pool users groups, soon to be supported by community and political activists started to hold public meetings against the closure, drawing substantial numbers in the process. From this the *Save Our Pool* campaign was launched with the goal not only of keeping the pool open but transforming its use as a health facility for all residents in Govanhill. The campaign sought to mobilise support from across the entire Govanhill community ... in the process drawing in people from very different cultural and religious backgrounds and from different age groups, political persuasions and different occupations. These included the Muslim Ladies Swimming Group, the Orthodox Jewish swimming groups, mother and toddler groups and the elderly ladies of Queen's Park Swimming Club.

...

'Save Our Pool' was not only about direct action through occupation and protest. With the support of local health officials and other local groups, campaign organisers were also keen to show that the pool could have a future and a new lease of life as a healthy living centre ...

The occupation was to end abruptly. 141 days following the start of the occupation it was forcibly ended by Sheriff Officers, acting for Glasgow City Council and supported by Strathclyde Police.

Mooney and Fyfe, 2006, pp. 141–4

Figure 5.3

Demonstrators demand that Glasgow City Council keep their hands off Govanhill Pool

Comment

Before considering the nature of the community mobilisation, it is important to note what the pool (or 'Calder Street Baths' as it was known locally) represented for the community. Mooney and Fyfe claim that the pool was symbolic of traditional tenemental life in Glasgow. By this they refer to the reliance across many generations of a large proportion of the city's working-class population on publicly provided washing and laundry facilities. Public baths, such as the kind typified by the Govanhill pool, offered leisure facilities, but their historical role was in some ways much more welfare oriented – providing the kinds of services that were either absent in the majority of Glasgow's poorer tenements or which ordinary working-class people could not afford to access elsewhere – and, of course, as a meeting place within a particular community setting.

As discussed in Chapters 1 and 3, such symbols are important both for identity and for community membership. Although different groups used the services separately, they came together to try to save the pool.

The extract also shows that the mobilisation went beyond a protest about closure. The community group was also transformative in that it brought together previously separated groups and in doing so was able to suggest ways in which new services could be developed. As discussed earlier, this might be interpreted as a community developing social capital and wanting to work in partnership with the local authority. The experiences of some of the campaigners support this:

> I have met so many people, you wouldn't believe. People that I didn't know were my neighbours and whom I hardly spoke to in the past. One example of what we've done is the garden in front of the pool. Before it was just a disused dumping ground. Volunteers got together and removed twenty bags of rubbish and needles. We painted the entire fence, planted flowers that were donated from local gardening businesses and built a wooden pagoda. There were street parties here, Sunday barbecues, a May feast, arts events. We have singsongs every Wednesday night [...] It's incredible. I have never seen a group like this, there are sub groups, there is a children committee, children are welcome at the public meetings.
>
> (Woman campaign member quoted in Bernatzky, 2001, cited in Mooney and Fyfe, 2006, p. 145)

> I have never been involved in a campaign like this in my life. It's incredibly creative; this campaign has got housewives, doctors, academics, homeless people, people with drug problems. It's a cross-section of the community life you wouldn't believe and look at this; we get on surprisingly well. I am really proud of people in Govanhill.
>
> (Male Asian student campaigner quoted in Bernatzky, 2001, cited in Mooney and Fyfe, 2006, p. 145)

However, local policymakers and agencies saw the campaign as being 'hijacked' by political elements with particular agendas reflected in its direct action tactics: 'While active communities that engage in "approved" forms of local action are to be welcomed, those who challenge the authority of local government can experience the full coercive force of the state' (Mooney and Fyfe, 2006, p. 147). The police claimed that 'a "violent minority" of "political agitators" had orchestrated a "riot"' in August 2001 outside the pool, during which five police officers were injured (Mooney and Fyfe, 2006, p. 144). In contrast, the campaigners argued that the Strathclyde Police and Glasgow City Council attempted to criminalise both the pool protestors and the Save Our Pool campaign itself.

This case study illustrates some of the conflicts and contradictions between, on the one hand, ideas of partnerships with active communities delivering policy and, on the other hand, grass-roots mobilisations that may act in opposition to policy. The campaign ultimately failed to stop the pool being closed. Although it had sought to go beyond the pool itself and suggest ways in which services in the area could be more broadly improved and developed, the campaign was not interpreted as evidence of valuable local bonding and bridging social capital. Instead, it was seen as an explicitly political – and given its tactics – *criminal* rather than *community* activity. We continue to address this issue in the following section.

4 Unruly acts: community activity challenging policymaking?

You have seen how community mobilisations can interact with, influence and, as in the example of the Govanhill campaign, oppose formal policy frames. In this final part of the chapter we develop our focus on what we have called 'unruly acts', by which we mean community activity that very explicitly and dramatically challenges policy frames and practices. The particular example we shall consider is that of 'urban unrest', and we ask here whether urban unrest can be understood and explained as community action or mobilisation by a 'troubled' population, or as a manifestation of social disorder by a 'trouble*some*' population. We also examine the ways in which, as a result of such urban unrest, communities can become the focus of governance as interventions are targeted at, and designed to manage, those perceived as 'problem populations' (see **Mooney, 2008**; Chapters 1, 2 and 4 in this volume).

4.1 Unruly acts: a long and transnational history

Violent disorder has a long history. As John Benyon (1987, p. 26) notes: 'in many respects this country's history appears remarkably turbulent with frequent outbursts of disorder. In the eighteenth century, civil commotion occurred over grievances such as the price of flour and bread, wages and conditions, political reform ... enclosures and turnpikes and excise duties'. Examples of such social unrest range from the Peasants' Revolt in 1381, the Gordon Riots in 1780, the Luddites in the 1800s, the Rebecca disorders in Wales in 1839, Tonypandy in 1910, Glasgow in 1919 through to the anti-poll tax riots of 1990. In the last quarter of the twentieth century, urban unrest in the UK took place predominantly in the early and mid 1980s in multicultural inner city areas of Bristol, London, Liverpool and Leeds. Smaller-scale outbreaks of unrest occurred in mainly white working-class suburban council housing

Figure 5.4

'Justice and truth for Larami and Moushin': a protest in a Paris suburb in 2007, following the deaths of two teenagers when their motorcycle crashed with a police car: their deaths sparked two nights of riots; urban unrest in Brixton, 1981; fires burning in Detroit during urban unrest, 1967 estates during the 1990s; for example, in Newcastle in 1991 and Luton in 1995. In 2001, major urban unrest took place in northern English towns and cities such as Bradford, Oldham and Burnley.

Bea Campbell argues that social unrest is 'what people do with their troubles and their anger' (Campbell, 1993, p. x). According to this view, unrest can be seen to be part of the way in which social inequality, poverty, alienation, hardship and despair are expressed. Unrest can be understood as community based because it incorporates a shared localism of what happens in particular places, but it can also be an articulation of a broader communal experience that is not tied to a single geographical place. For example, the urban unrest in the UK in 1981 began in Brixton but spread to other cities where local multicultural communities recognised the same grievances and responded in a similar way.

Community-related urban unrest is not a phenomenon confined to the UK. An obvious example is the urban unrest that was a feature of numerous US cities during the 1960s (see Abu-Lughod, 2007). Among the most significant of these were the Harlem Riot of 1964, the Watts Riot of 1965 and the Detroit Riot of 1967. These civil disorders were about community in that they were a geographically based community action, but they can also be understood as being about communities of shared identity and experience: in this case, as African Americans (see the discussion of community as place and identity in Chapter 1).

In 2005 and 2007, France experienced extensive urban unrest in the suburbs of Paris and in cities such as Toulouse, where communities of French Arab and North African origin are concentrated (see **Mooney, 2008**; Wacquant, 2008). As in the unrest of the 1980s and 2000s in the UK, and in the USA in the 1960s, the unrest in France can be linked to notions of community via a particular localism and broader identity politics. In 2005, Nikolas Sarkozy (who was then the Interior Minister and was subsequently elected as Prime Minister of France in 2007) denied suggestions that deprivation, social exclusion and racism had prompted the unrest. He condemned those who took part in it as criminals and condemned the unrest as a series of criminal acts to be dealt with by tougher police action.

Benyon (1987, pp. 26–7) argues that there are three competing perspectives that explain urban unrest. The *first* of these is the conservative perspective; Sarkozy's response to the unrest in Paris and other French cities represents this. This view denies any legitimacy to disorder and, as Benyon notes, interprets disorder 'as an aberration perpetrated by irresponsible and criminal elements who may be motivated by greed and excitement'.

Activity 5.4

As an example of the conservative perspective, read through the headlines reporting urban unrest in the UK in 2001, as shown in Figure 5.5. Consider the ways in which notions of criminality and illegality are conveyed to audiences in the language used.

Figure 5.5
Media headlines relating to urban unrest in Bradford in 2001

Comment

Media reports of such events, which use a language of 'mindless destruction', 'sheer criminality', 'vile orgy of violence', 'thugs' and 'bloody riot', present a particular narrative of those people and communities involved (as in the case of official responses to some of the Govanhill pool protestors, which we discussed earlier). It is important to note that the various terms used to analyse these events, such as 'urban unrest', 'violent disorder', 'riot' or 'uprising', all carry nuanced and different political meanings that convey the political legitimacy or otherwise of the unrest. The language with which unrest is categorised also has juridical consequences. For example, according to McGhee (2003), the official classification of the 2001 Bradford disturbances as 'riot' rather than 'violent disorder', which was used in the Burnley and Oldham disturbances, had implications for sentencing. Under the Public Order Act 1986, 'violent disorder' carries a maximum sentence of five years, compared with a charge of 'riot', which carries a maximum sentence of ten years (Worley, 2005). From this perspective, unrest is reduced to predominantly simple acts of illegality and linked to notions of 'dysfunctional' or 'problem' communities that require targeted crime control interventions.

The *second perspective* on unrest highlighted by Benyon relates to the liberal or welfarist explanation, which focuses on social issues such as poverty, unemployment, declining industry, poor housing and education provision, racism and political and social marginalisation. Benyon identifies the *third perspective* as a radical one in that it 'interprets collective violence as purposeful, structured and politically meaningful. It is seen as a normal, legitimate and effective means of protest by groups who have no other opportunities' (Benyon, 1987, p. 27). For example, this interpretation is reflected in the work of the social theorist A. Sivanandan who commented, in relation to the 1980s urban unrest in the UK, that:

> Nowhere have the youth, black and white, identified their problems with unemployment alone. ... They know, viscerally, that there will be no work for them, ever, no call for their labour ...

> They are not the unemployed, but the never employed. ... Theirs is a different hunger – a hunger to retain the freedom, the life-style, the dignity which they have carved out from the stone of their lives.
> (Sivanandan, 1982, p. 150)

These very different interpretations of unrest and community mobilisations reflect the uneasy boundaries between social welfare and crime control policymaking and practice. For instance, the criminal justice system, politicians of the political centre and the right and some sections of the media tend to work with conservative approaches to unrest, whereas the liberal view tends to inform those of the political centre and the left, community organisations and some sections of the media. A mix of both these perspectives was reflected in the reports and inquiries into some of the disturbances mentioned here. It is these policy responses that we now consider.

4.2 Themes in the policy responses to urban unrest

In the wake of the US riots in the 1960s, the Report of the Kerner Commission (1968) called for the addition of one million government-created jobs, the institution of a higher minimum wage, significantly increased welfare benefits, and more resources for education and housing. The Kerner Report can be viewed as a welfarist or liberal policy response in that the riots were explained predominantly in terms of social causes. Like the Kerner Report, the Scarman Report (1981), into the Brixton disorders in the early 1980s, generally also took a welfarist view, although it did maintain some elements of the conservative perspective. While the Scarman Inquiry found that the police were not institutionally racist (as had been claimed by protestors), the report highlighted that a largely 'white' police force policing ethnically and culturally diverse communities was a concern, and suggested that some police officers would benefit from further training in community and race relations (McLaughlin, 2007). Alongside his recommendations around policing, Scarman also addressed issues of racial discrimination within education, housing and employment, and political alienation. For example, it is particularly pertinent to our interests in this chapter that Scarman concluded that 'local communities should be more fully involved in the decisions that affect them. A "top down" approach to regeneration does not seem to have worked' (Scarman, 1981, para. 2.36).

In the most recent reports into outbreaks of urban unrest in the UK, the liberal view is still in evidence, but the emphasis on the communities involved in the unrest has become more pronounced. A number of policy reports were produced over a very short period of time, all related to urban unrest in northern English towns and cities in 2001. The Ouseley Report (2001) was produced before the disturbances, but investigated the issues of diversity in Bradford. The Cantle Report (Home Office, 2001a) was produced after the urban unrest in Bradford. In the same year, reports relating to disturbances in Burnley (The Clarke Report, Home Office, 2001b) and Oldham (The Ritchie Report, Home Office, 2001c) were published. The Denham Report (Home Office, 2001d) was the government response to the previous four reports and provided an overview of the urban unrest in Bradford, Burnley and Oldham.

Activity 5.5

In this activity we ask you to read an extract from an official government policy report. As you do so, think about the following questions:

■ What are seen as the causes of the unrest?

■ In what ways is the concept of community being identified?

■ What solutions are proposed?

The extract comes from the Cantle Report into disturbances in Bradford in 2001.

Extract 5.2

Whilst the physical segregation of housing estates and inner city areas came as no surprise, the team was particularly struck by the depth of polarisation of our towns and cities. The extent to which these physical divisions were compounded by so many other aspects of our daily lives, was very evident. Separate educational arrangements, community and voluntary bodies, employment, places of worship, language, social and cultural networks, means that many communities operate on the basis of a series of parallel lives. These lives often do not seem to touch at any point, let alone overlap and promote any meaningful interchanges.

A Muslim of Pakistani origin summed this up:

'When I leave this meeting with you I will go home and not see another white face until I come back here next week'

Similarly, a young man from a white council estate said:

'I never met anyone on this estate who wasn't like us from around here'.

... We believe that there is an urgent need to promote community cohesion, based upon a greater knowledge of, contact between, and respect for, the various cultures that now make Great Britain such a rich and diverse nation.

It is also essential to establish a greater sense of citizenship, based on (a few) common principles which are shared and observed by all sections of the community. This concept of citizenship would also place a higher value on cultural differences.

Home Office, 2001a, pp. 9–10

Comment

The physical and social segregation of the different communities was seen as the major cause of the unrest, and following these events in 2001 a degree of consensus emerged about the problem of segregated communities; the way forward that was proposed in the policy reports was to build 'cohesive communities'. This emphasis on the importance of cohesion, integration and commonality, rather than the valuing of cultural diversity and difference, has since come to dominate debates about multiculture (see Cantle, 2008; Chapters 1, 3 and 6 in this volume).

The issue of segregated communities has been raised as a problem in all the official reports produced after the UK riots of 2001. To understand the way that cities such as Bradford have become segregated involves unravelling the housing policies of earlier periods, which helped to create these polarised communities. The Cantle Report recognised that sometimes families chose to live close together for reasons of support, but that sometimes polarisation was more to do with housing allocation policies and economic constraints. The welfare–crime entanglement becomes visible when we see how social welfare policies, in this example in relation to housing, have helped to create segregated communities. This segregation is then blamed as one of the main causes of the urban unrest.

The issues relating to 'ethnic segregation' were discussed extensively following the events in Bradford, Burnley and Oldham (Home Office, 2001a, 2001b, 2001c, 2001d; Ouseley, 2001). The level of policy and political concern with the notion of segregated ethnic communities has meant that these reports have been influential in driving through a new language of community cohesion, which has replaced an earlier language of celebrating multicultural diversity. Paul Bagguley and Yasmin Hussain (2006) note that this emphasis on community cohesion and ethnic segregation has meant that these became *the* dominant framework for interpreting and responding to the unrest. Consequently, there has been little room for the consideration of how segregation based on other social relations, such as class and material inequalities, may have shaped the events of 2001.

The challenge provided by gender further complicates, disrupts and unsettles the 'traditional' accounts of urban unrest. For example, the 2001 UK disturbances were commonly seen as clashes between young Muslim men and the police, or between young Muslim men and young white men. This forms part of the reimagining of community as a problem in gendered and racialised terms (Alexander, 2004). The Ouseley Report (2001) referred to the difficulty of accessing the views of young Asian women and teenage girls within Bradford. Anecdotal evidence of gender inequalities was presented in the Cantle Report. The Denham Report also argued that it was concerned in particular with those cultural practices that denied women the right to participate as equal citizens (Home Office, 2001d). The worry was expressed that it was difficult to hear the views of women and girls from the communities concerned. We will explore this issue of gender further by using contrasting evidence from social policy sources and a biographical account.

Activity 5.6

Read Extracts 5.3 and 5.4 below. The first comes from the Denham Report and the second is one woman's account of the way in which women mobilised during an earlier period of urban unrest in Bradford in 1995. As you read the extracts, consider the way in which biographical evidence is different from that offered by policy reports.

Extract 5.3

The reports of Cantle, Clarke, Ritchie and Ouseley bring to life the feelings, views and aspirations of all the local communities in areas where there were disturbances. Cantle makes comparisons with communities whose experience had been much more positive. The Ministerial Group is clear that we must listen to and involve local people in developing policies which meet their needs. Young people of all communities must be included, as must women, and Muslim women in particular, whose voice has not been heard clearly so far. Initiating a wide and open debate around the issues raised in this report is, we believe, the essential next step.

Home Office, 2001d, p. 4

Extract 5.4

A group of eight women – four Asian and four white – decided to go out onto the street with a message of peace to try and calm down the situation and prevent further violence.

Most of us were members of an Interfaith Women for Peace group. This group is currently made up of Asian and white women from Bradford who have been meeting in each other's homes for the past year to discuss ... how to promote cross-cultural understanding and racial justice at the local level. Having this kind of network enabled us to contact each other quickly and to be assured that we would all be in favour of such an action.

By about 11.30pm we had all met at the home of one of the women who lives very near to where the trouble first began. We made a banner from a sheet, with 'peace' in English, Urdu, and Arabic and decided that would be our main message: we were making a plea to stop the violence. ... We intended to call for an inquiry and for talks to get to the heart of the problem.

Because the crowd was all male, and because the violence on both sides (youth and police) had been perpetrated by men, we felt that women's presence on the street would be a powerful statement. We planned to walk up to the police station and back with the banner and see what effect we could have. ...

As we walked up Oak Lane, we began to see just how large the crowd of men was. Several of the youth called out 'You should be ashamed – go back home!' or 'We respect you – but go home!' Other men took on the role of protectors, helping us to cross the street with the banner and opening the way for us ...

... It appeared to us that this action had dissipated the tension, at least temporarily, and there was no violence that night.

The next day we found ourselves briefly mentioned on the national news and on the front page of the local newspaper with the headline 'We must heal these wounds.' The image of women in the streets holding a peace banner clearly expressed what many felt. Though our action was brief, it did seem to have an impact, and it was personally empowering for all of us.

Peace News, 1995

Comment

Extract 5.4 is an example of biographical evidence. Biography involves a personal account or perspective on an issue. It is often individual and more informal in presentation than that presented in more 'official' sources such as policy reports. When we read biographical evidence we often have an emotional response to the narrator, who is usually telling a personal story. Biographical evidence, together with oral history testimony, is often the only way of accessing some information about an event. In this way, these accounts add further richness and depth to our understanding of events. In this example, the views are of one woman involved in a peace march in Bradford and shows how women from different ethnic communities were working together. Since the official

Figure 5.6
Women peace marchers
in Bradford

reports had considered that the views of women were often absent or difficult to access (see Extract 5.3, for example), seeking out other forms of evidence may be necessary.

What other kinds of evidence were also absent from the policy reports and how could these have been accessed? The views of children and young people are often marginalised, but initiatives such as Youth Parliaments, which exist in Bradford, attempted to redress this by involving children and young people in issues of local governance following the riots (O'Toole and Gale, 2006). For example, children and young people have reported through the Youth Parliament that they are concerned about issues such as drugs, (gun) crime, transport and racism (Rashid, 2007).

In this section we have looked at activities in communities that are commonly constructed as problematic – riots or urban unrest. We have seen how communities involved in unrest are ambivalently viewed as dysfunctional and dangerous and as vulnerable and marginal. The tendency in the reports is to 'diagnose' the unrest as communities in need of governance, rather than as community actions reacting to perceived inequalities and seeking social justice. Unlike some of the community actions that we examined in Section 3, urban unrest is not seen as presenting a form of social capital that can be linked into the policy system.

5   Review

This chapter has explored a diverse range of community practices, activities and mobilisations. It has considered how people enact community through everyday and mundane acts of social care. These informal social interactions may themselves constitute small acts of welfare and are seen by policymakers as crucial for social cohesion and stability. In examining a series of examples, the chapter then suggested that community activities can become more systematically and formally organised, and may either interact with and influence policy agendas and lead to the establishment of new services or facilities, or attempt (successfully or unsuccessfully) to save existing services and networks of social support. The outcome of community mobilisations may go beyond very specific goals and foster new understandings and recognition of needs for services. Indeed, community mobilisations demonstrate ways in which community can shape policy rather than simply being the object of policy.

Through the question of the relationship between community activity and policy frames, the chapter has examined urban unrest as an extended example of a policy-challenging form of community mobilisation. We have suggested that urban unrest constitutes community action given that it combines a shared experience of social grievance, exclusion or hardship, and that this has both spatial and identity dimensions. In other words, urban unrest can be a response to processes and/or events happening in a particular place, and/or a response formed through a shared sense of identity that goes beyond any specific place. The focus on urban unrest has also allowed us to see a very specific entanglement between social welfare and crime control interventions, because policy responses to the dramatic and high-profile nature of urban unrest have tended to stress either the criminality of the action and those involved, or the need to address the social welfare issues that may be perceived to be the causes of the disorder. In our consideration of the various reports that resulted from inquiries into urban unrest, we have seen that these two approaches are not necessarily mutually exclusive (the Scarman Report, for example). We have also seen how, in the UK since the early 2000s, the notion of building community cohesion has emerged as a key policy response to disorder and cultural diversity.

Drawing on a wide range of qualitative and quantitative evidence and sources – social science research; reports and policy texts; media; personal accounts – our discussion of community mobilisations has reinforced a central theme of this book: that the concept of community is contradictory and contested. In emphasising its turbulence and stressing that community is not just the object of policy, this chapter has shown that community is also what people 'do' and the basis on which they may act. The chapter has examined this enactment and its policy relationship mainly in the context of the UK, but it has sought to suggest that this goes beyond national boundaries and has indicated the ways in which we can see community being enacted in transnational and international ways (see also Chapters 3, 4 and 6). While the chapter has suggested that the notion of social capital offers helpful ways of analysing bottom-up community actions, it has also urged some caution with the concept and highlighted how only certain forms of social capital may be valued by policymakers. Indeed, as the community cohesion agenda demonstrates, some mobilisations are seen to constitute 'too much community'.

Because the concept of community is meaningful in terms of how people choose to act, there are a number of instances in which this 'enacted' community connects with the broader relationship between social welfare and crime control policies. For example, this chapter has shown how:

■ what people 'do' can be understood as representing informal and formalised social care

■ community activity may often be focused around crime control and safety issues

■ the idea of cohesive communities is attached to attempts to reduce crime and social harm

■ community activity may not always be welcomed, and may be viewed as problematic by policymakers

■ community mobilisations can constitute criminal activity and social disorder, but also highlight issues of social division, inequality and injustice.

It is this multiplicity in the ways in which community can be and is enacted that has been the concern of this chapter.

Further reading

The Roots of Urban Unrest by John Benyon and John Solomos (1987, Pergamon Press) offers a useful and insightful edited collection reviewing the debates about how to understand urban disorder in the UK in the 1980s, and an assessment of the interventions made in response to outbreaks of disorder. Ted Cantle's *Community Cohesion: A New Framework for Race and Diversity* (2008, Palgrave) offers an updated discussion of the findings of the original report and includes an extended discussion of the concept of community cohesion. Anne Power and Helen Willmot's *Social Capital within the Neighbourhood* (2007, Centre for Analysis of Social Exclusion) provides a full account of the study discussed in the early part of the chapter and examines the usefulness of the concept of social capital in deprived neighbourhoods.

References

Abu-Lughod, J.L. (2007) *Race, Space and Riots in Chicago, New York, and Los Angeles*, Oxford, Oxford University Press.

Alexander, C. (2004) 'Imagining the Asian gang: ethnicity, masculinity and youth after "the riots"', *Critical Social Policy*, vol. 24, no. 4, pp. 526–49.

Bagguley, P. and Hussain, Y. (2006) 'Conflict and cohesion: official constructions of "community" around the 2001 riots in Britain' in Herbrechter, S. and Higgins, M. (eds) 'Returning (to) communities: theory, culture and political practice of the communal', *Critical Studies*, vol. 28, Amsterdam, New York.

Benyon, J. (1987) 'Interpretations of civil disorder' in Benyon, J. and Solomos, J. (eds) *The Roots of Urban Unrest*, Oxford, Pergamon Press.

Bogside and Brandywell Women's Group (undated) *About Us* [online], http://freederry.org/bbwg/aboutus.htm (Accessed 9 January 2008).

Campbell, B. (1993) *Goliath: Britain's Dangerous Places*, London, Methuen.

Cantle, T. (2008) *Community Cohesion: A New Framework for Race and Diversity* London, Palgrave.

Coulthard, M., Walker, A. and Morgan, A. (2002) *People's Perceptions of Their Neighbourhood and Community Involvement: Results from the Social Capital Module of the General Household Survey 2000*, London, National Statistics; also available online at http://www.statistics.gov.uk/pdfdir/nci0602.pdf (Accessed 26 November 2007).

Crawford, A. (2004) 'People of Shetland unite to save failed asylum-seekers from deportation', *Sunday Herald*, 11 April [online], http://www.irr.org.uk/sad/articles/shetland.html (Accessed 11 July 2008).

Cresswell, T. (2004) *Place: A Short Introduction*, Oxford, Blackwell.

Fisher, J. (1993) *Out of the Shadows: Women, Resistance and Politics in South America*, London, Latin America Bureau.

Home Office (2001a) *Community Cohesion: A Report of the Independent Review Team* (The Cantle Report), London, The Stationery Office.

Home Office (2001b) *The Report of the Burnley Task Force* (The Clarke Report), London, The Stationery Office.

Home Office (2001c) *The Oldham Independent Review* (The Ritchie Report), London, The Stationery Office.

Home Office (2001d) *Building Cohesive Communities* (The Denham Report), London, The Stationery Office.

Home Office (2008) *What is Neighbourhood Watch?* [online], http://www.crimereduction.homeoffice.gov.uk/neighbourhoodwatch/nwatch09.htm (Accessed 11 July 2008).

Humphries, P. (2000) 'Town protests over asylum hostel plan', *The Guardian*, 20 December [online], http://www.guardian.co.uk/society/2000/dec/20/asylum (Accessed 27 November 2007).

Kerner, O. (1968) *The 1968 Report of the National Advisory Commission on Civil Disorder* (The Kerner Report), United States Kerner Commission.

McGhee, D. (2003) 'Moving to "our" common ground – a critical examination of community cohesion discourse in twenty-first century Britain', *Sociological Review*, vol. 51, no. 3, pp. 376–404.

McLaughlin, E. (2007) *The New Policing*, London, Sage.

Make Poverty History (undated) [online], http://www.makepovertyhistory.org/ (Accessed 12 May 2008).

Martin, D.G. (2003) '"Place-framing" as place-making: constituting neighborhood for organizing and activism', *Annals of the Association of American Geographers*, vol. 93, no. 3, pp. 730–50.

Mooney, G. (2008) '"Problem" populations, "problem" places' in Newman, J. and Yeates, N. (eds) *Social Justice: Welfare, Crime and Society*, Maidenhead, Open University Press/Milton Keynes, The Open University.

Mooney, G. and Fyfe, N. (2006) 'New Labour and community protests: the case of the Govanhill Swimming Pool Campaign, Glasgow', *Local Economy*, vol. 21, no. 2, pp. 137–51.

Moseley, M.J. and Pahl, R.E. (2007) *Social Capital in Rural Places: A Report to Defra*, London, The Stationery Office.

Neal, S. and Agyeman, J. (2006) 'Remaking English ruralities' in Neal, S. and Agyeman, J. (eds) *The New Countryside: Ethnicity, Nation and Exclusion in Contemporary Rural Britain*, Bristol, The Policy Press.

Newman, J. and Yeates, N. (eds) (2008) *Social Justice: Welfare, Crime and Society*, Maidenhead, Open University Press/Milton Keynes, The Open University.

O'Toole, T. and Gale, R. (2006) 'Participative governance and youth inclusion: the case of youth parliaments', paper presented to Theorising Children's Participation: International and interdisciplinary Perspectives, University of Edinburgh, 4–6 September.

Ouseley, H. (2001) *Community Pride not Prejudice* (The Ouseley Report), Bradford Vision, Bradford City Council.

Peace News (1995) 'Responding to a riot', *Peace News*, no. 2393, August [online], http://www.peacenews.info/issues/2393/pn239312.htm (Accessed 11 July 2008).

Power, A. and Willmot, H. (2007) *Social Capital within the Neighbourhood*, London, Centre for Analysis of Social Exclusion.

Putnam, R. (2003) 'The prosperous community: social capital and public life', *The American Prospect*, vol. 4, no. 13, pp. 35–42.

Rashid, N. (2007) 'Engaging with Bradford & Keighley Youth Parliament', presentation to seminar; Participation and Wellbeing in Civil Society: How Children and Young People Win Friends and Influence People, Bradford University, 6 November.

Scarman, L. (1981) *The Brixton Disorders, 10–12 April 1981* (The Scarman Report), London, HMSO.

Schools Against Deportation (2005) [online], http://www.irr.org.uk/sad/index.html (Accessed 12 May 2008).

Sivanandan, A. (1982) 'From resistance to rebellion: Asian and Afro-Caribbean struggles in Britain', *Race and Class*, vol. XXIII, no. 2/3, pp. 111–52.

Taylor, M. (2003) *Public Policy in the Community*, Basingstoke, Palgrave Macmillan.

Wacquant, L. (2008) *Urban Outcasts*, Cambridge, Polity Press.

Worley, C. (2005) '"It's not about race. It's about the community": New Labour and "community cohesion"', *Critical Social Policy*, vol. 25, no. 4, pp. 483–96.

Chapter 6
Conclusion

Gerry Mooney and Sarah Neal

Contents

1   Introduction

The previous five chapters have taken you on a diverse journey through the ways in which the concept of community can be understood and has been mobilised by social theorists and academics, governments and politicians, policymakers and practitioners across a range of social welfare and crime control sites. Last, but very far from least, we have seen how community makes sense to people in their everyday lives and how people take social action on the basis of it. We hope it is now clear why, early in Chapter 1, we spoke of a sociological 'health warning' needing to accompany any use of the concept of community. What the multiple meanings attached to community reflect is the complex social world in which issues of identity, belonging, affection, affiliation, care, safety, stability, order, regulation and exclusion are all able to intersect and converge. The key task of this chapter is to review why community retains its currency and popularity as a theoretical, political, policy and everyday concept. The chapter does this by casting its gaze back across the previous chapters in three main ways:

- First, it reminds you of the key aims of the book, which were set out in Chapter 1, and explores the ways in which the chapters address and respond to these.

- Second, it considers the role that evidence has played in theoretical, political and, particularly, policy interpretations of the concept of community.

- Third, it re-examines exactly how and why a focus on community helps make sense of the leaky relationship between social welfare and crime control policy domains.

Figure 6.1
The convergence of welfare, crime and community: Strathclyde Police illuminated advertisement at Glasgow Airport, May 2008

2 Revisiting the key aims of the book

Chapter 1 explained that *Community* would address five interconnected aims. These were to:

- examine the *different meanings* attached to the concept of community and the debates as to its definitions

- explore why the concept of community has such *positive associations* and *widespread appeal*

- understand how community can be used to identify 'problem populations' *and* as the basis for responding to such populations

- look at some of the ways in which community has played a *significant role* in social welfare policy and crime control policy

- discuss how the concept of community has been researched in the social sciences, and consider how policymakers have *engaged with evidence* about communities.

Activity 6.1

We can look at Table 6.1 and see at a glance how each of the five chapters could be mapped on to these five aims. However, it is more useful to think about this mapping process through a review of the content of particular chapters.

Can you think of examples from the material you have encountered in any of the five previous chapters that would substantiate or more fully explain any of the ticks in Table 6.1? Which chapter(s) particularly responded to which particular aim(s)?

Table 6.1 Brief overview of the relationship between the book chapters and the book aims

	Aim 1	Aim 2	Aim 3	Aim 4	Aim 5
Chapter 1	✓	✓	✓		✓
Chapter 2	✓		✓	✓	✓
Chapter 3	✓	✓			✓
Chapter 4			✓	✓	✓
Chapter 5		✓		✓	✓

Comment

You may, for example, have thought that Chapter 1 in particular considered the different ways in which community has been defined when it argued that place and locality, identity and cultural bonds, boundaries and exclusions, order and regulation could all be used as apparently distinct lenses through which to understand what community might mean. Chapter 1 suggested that these differences gave community its contested status, but it also argued that perhaps these differences were not as great as they may initially seem and that they relate to and reinforce each other.

You may have identified Chapter 3 as addressing the question of community's positive associations. Here John Clarke developed some of the arguments introduced in the first chapter, particularly in his discussion of the desire for community and ways of securing community – through gated community living for example. With its focus on social order, Chapter 3 examined why community comes to be mobilised in terms of how people imagine social bonds and feeling safe, secure and cared for, and it considered a number of sites with which a welfare-orientated, neighbourly, 'golden age' notion of community – the rural village community and the 'traditional' working-class community – is associated.

You may have selected Chapter 5 for its engagement with ways in which community shapes how people choose to act socially and collectively around a range of issues and social resources. The ways in which people identify themselves and feel affiliated to others can lead to mobilisations, actions and campaigns to influence policy. Sharon Pinkney and Esther Saraga spent time in their chapter discussing how community is enacted and practised in informal and everyday settings.

Chapters 2 and 4 were specifically concerned with the questions regarding community-associated social problems and community-based social welfare and crime control policymaking. Chapter 2 looked in detail at how community has been used in policymaking and interventions in a range of ways, as Allan Cochrane and Janet Newman's discussion of the five advertisements for different types of community-based posts demonstrated. They also considered the ways in which community has been mobilised as a strategy for welfare interventions in UK and global settings, and suggested that community is increasingly replacing national government as the primary site of policy thinking and service delivery. Chapter 4 extended some of these same themes in relation to its focus on the ways in which communities are governed through what Gordon Hughes has called a hybrid (i.e. social welfare and crime control) policy field. With a focus on broader notions of social harm, on multi-agency approaches and on community participation, crime and disorder

Figure 6.2

Remembering a golden age of community? Children playing in London streets in the 1950s; and a London street party, 1945

reduction partnerships (CDRPs) and community safety partnerships (CSPs) capture perfectly the convergences between community, social welfare and crime control policies.

Chapter 2's focus on antisocial behaviour, Chapter 3's examination of the tensions in the contemporary East End of London, Chapter 4's discussion of Aboriginal-Australian populations and community safety approaches, and Chapter 5's discussion of policy responses to urban unrest can all be understood as examples of a direct engagement with the question as to why 'community' is being used both to describe and identify particular social problems *and* as the basis through which to counter those social problems.

You may have thought of examples from all the chapters to support the fifth question regarding evidence and research on communities. Each chapter includes discussion of a range of evidence regarding the concept of community and the ways in which policymakers have integrated evidence into policy formulation and implementation. Gordon Hughes, in Chapter 4, for example, provided quantitative data on the evaluation of the community safety policy. Similarly, in Chapter 2 Allan Cochrane and Janet Newman examined the qualitative-based inquiries into the success or otherwise of antisocial behaviour initiatives in relation to behaviour in public places and social housing tenancy agreements. Sharon Pinkney and Esther Saraga, in Chapter 5, discussed the ways in which the findings from government inquiries into urban unrest – such as the Cantle Report – shaped future policy interventions.

It is the ways in which evidence about or on communities has been mobilised and represented in each chapter that we now want to consider in further detail.

3   Community, evidence and policy

Across the chapters in this book you have encountered various examples and discussions of evidence and communities. The chapters have diversely revealed the ways in which social scientists and policymakers have gathered and collected data both to extend understandings of the concept of community and of community practices, and to evaluate the need for, and the effectiveness of, particular community-based policies.

Activity 6.2

Table 6.2 provides an overview of some of the types of evidence you have encountered in the previous chapters.

We have listed just one example of evidence from each chapter, and the table requires that we identify the evidence as belonging in one column or another. Can you think of other examples of evidence from the chapters you have read? How would you enter them into this kind of table? Can you think of examples of evidence in which you might 'tick' all the columns? As you reflect on this, be aware that the delineations between types of evidence are not necessarily precise or mutually exclusive.

Table 6.2 Brief overview of some of the different types of evidence discussed in the book chapters

	Qualitative research	Quantitative research	Social theory focus	Evaluation focus	Policy-related focus
Chapter 1 example: Chávez study	✓		✓		
Chapter 2 example: Prior et al. studies	✓		✓	✓	✓
Chapter 3 example: Dench et al. study	✓		✓		✓
Chapter 4 example: Home Office and Audit Commission study of CDRPs		✓		✓	✓
Chapter 5 example: Cantle Report	✓			✓	✓

Comment

A number of examples may have occurred to you. You may have thought of some of the focus group interview data collected in Sarah Neal and Sue Walters's study of rural populations, or Mike Savage's figures on local senses of belonging in Manchester, from Chapter 1. You may have recalled the 'Shoreditch Our Way' report from Chapter 2, or Setha Low's research on gated communities and Young and Willmott's 1957 study of Bethnal Green in East London, in Chapter 3. Thinking of examples of evidence in Chapter 4, you may have remembered Gordon Hughes's discussion of Harry Blagg's research on Aboriginal social exclusion, and Chapter 5 provides a range of different examples – for instance, Gerry Mooney and Nick Fyfe's investigation of the local community actions to save Govanhill Swimming Pool in Glasgow, and the Power and Willmot study of social capital in four deprived urban neighbourhoods in England.

All of these (and many others) could be appropriately added into Table 6.2, although their categorisation as qualitative, quantitative, social theory focused, evaluation focused and primarily policy related may prove more challenging or not definitively clear. In part, this is a reflection of the diverse interpretations of community – these research examples variously work with community as place based or identity based, as being about boundaries or about managing populations. The challenges of categorising evidence act as a reminder of the different research methods and the different research and policy agendas that may surround the investigation of communities and related social welfare and crime control interventions.

 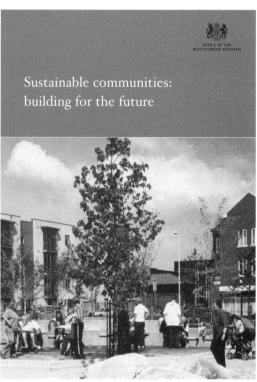

Figure 6.3
Government reports are one source of evidence for research into communities and community policy: *Communities First Guidance 2007*, published by the Welsh Assembly Government in 2007, and *Sustainable Communities: Building for the Future*, published by The Office of the Deputy Prime Minister of the UK Government in 2003

These challenges also in part reflect the slippery relationship between quantitative and qualitative research approaches. The two are not always as distinct as they might appear; for example, research that is qualitative will include a quantitative element in that it will also be interested in the repeated or shared patterns of findings even if the sample size is very small. Similarly, quantitative research methods may incorporate aspects of qualitative methods and attempt to try to find out the experiences, perspectives and explanations behind statistical findings. Chapter 4 included discussion of this in relation to the Home Office and Audit Commission findings into the effectiveness of community safety partnerships. Gordon Hughes made the point that statistical data demonstrating successful or unsuccessful crime reduction and prevention partnerships and target achievements may provide only a limited explanatory picture of effective policy implementation. Hughes suggested that evaluative research approaches need to be able to engage with more complex sets of tensions between narrowly defined crime reduction figures and broader socio-economic factors in deciding what does or does not work in a particular geographical location, and why or why not. This is also a reminder of the importance of understanding that evidence is sought and gathered in often complex social contexts (see also Chapter 3; **Cochrane and Talbot, 2008**).

The discussion of evidence in Chapter 4 shows some of the strengths and limitations of, and overlaps between, different research methods, and provides an opportunity to see the tensions between social science or academic-based research and evaluative or 'what works' research.

Again, Table 6.2 indicates that it is possible to locate research in one or the other of these categories, but in our discussion here it is becoming clear that there may be a substantial amount of overlap between academic research and evaluative research. Can we clearly delineate the work of Prior et al., detailed in Chapter 2, into one or other category? Probably not, given that it has its roots in, and is relevant to, both domains. Similarly, if we recall Chapter 3's discussion of the study by Dench et al., of the 'new East End' in London, we may identify it as an academic or a social science piece of research, but it is also clear that it will be of interest to, and could inform, both local policymakers and practitioners as well as politicians, given its focus on the social relations of urban multiculture, notions of Britishness and competition over a range of welfare resources (e.g. around housing). If we think back to Chapter 1's discussion of social capital and the work of Robert Putnam and Amitai Etzioni, we can see how the work of social theorists has been influential in political thinking and policy development and, as Chapter 5 noted, how the interest in social capital is reflected in the extent of research – the Health Development Agency study, for example – which seeks to investigate it. This shows that research and ideas do not flow in one direction. Chapter 5's discussion of urban unrest and the policy-orientated inquiries into this, such as the Scarman Report in 1981 and the Cantle Report in 2001, show not only that these have been central policy drivers, but also that they have been the subject of interest, scrutiny and analysis by academics and social researchers. What, then, can we conclude from this discussion on evidence and policy?

- First, although we may be able to place evidence into discrete categories, these are not absolute and the boundaries between quantitative and qualitative may be blurred and mixed, or multi-methods may be used in research design so that both approaches are able to complement each other.

- Second, research and data collection may or may not be easily definable as academic or evaluative. The boundaries between the two may be leaky and the audiences for either type of research may not be limited to policymakers or practitioners or politicians or social scientists. It is important to recognise that there is a certain amount of dialogue and conversation between and across these different audiences.

■ Third, evidence is often highly charged or politicised – think back, for example, to Chapter 4's discussion of the *Little Children Are Sacred* report and the National Emergency Response Bill in Australia. Some evidence might be selected and other evidence ignored to support particular policy interventions. This highlights the difficulties and tensions that surround attempts to reconcile the multiple meanings and understandings of community pursued by academics and other researchers with the *politics* of policymaking.

■ The fourth, and perhaps most important, point to make refers not only to the extent of research (of many different kinds) into community and communities, but also to the stretch or elasticity of the concept of community. Such stretching is, as we have seen in different chapters, apparent across the social sciences, policy, political and everyday contexts, and also occurs across different national contexts and within both historical and contemporary settings. In other words, what we particularly want to stress here is that it is possible to see a chain of connections between (a) community as a social science concept; (b) the production of evidence and research on community; and (c) policymaking that centres on particular mobilisations of ideas and notions of community. This is not to say that this chain is coherent and systematic – rather, we would insist that it is often highly complex, interrupted and contradictory – but it is to assert that there is a set of (often uncertain) relationships between community, research and policy interventions.

Activity 6.3

It might make more sense to try to draw this set of relationships visually in order to highlight some of the complexities between them.

Have a look at Figure 6.4. Think about the directions of influence between community, personal lives, evidence, policymaking and social order, and insert direction arrows to demonstrate the ways in which each impacts on and shapes the other.

Figure 6.4
Connecting community, research, personal lives, politics and policy

Research and evidence

Personal lives
and social action   Community   Policymaking
                                                                   and policy delivery

Politics and social order

Comment

Although this may look straightforward, as soon as an attempt is made to map coherent links on to it, it actually becomes quite difficult to decide on the order of impact and influence, as Figure 6.5 shows. Perhaps this difficulty in itself reflects the messy and turbulent terrains in which the concept of community, policymaking and research agendas interact and influence each other.

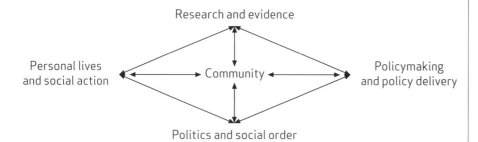

Figure 6.5
The multiple connections between community, research, personal lives, politics and policy interventions

What each of the chapters in this book has shown are aspects of this turbulence, but each has also, and very importantly, demonstrated the *proximity* (if not the coherence) between community, evidence, policy interventions, politics and the everyday. In other words, we may not be able to find a clear-cut set of relations between all of these, but we can argue that they can be bundled together in some, albeit unstable, forms of alignment. Let us consider briefly two examples of policy interventions that reflect this proximity. The first is taken from *Our Shared Future* (2007), the report from the Commission on Integration and Cohesion. You may recall that the report – in which community is a key concept – featured in Chapters 1 and 2.

Figure 6.6
Contemporary urban multiculture: Whitechapel High Street, London, 2005

The Commission was set up by the government's Communities Minister, as an expert working party with a twelve-month lifetime, in order to examine identity, diversity and social cohesion after the bombings in London in July 2005. The Report is itself a substantial document. Extract 6.1 below reproduces part of the Commission's Foreword.

Extract 6.1

A strong theme running through this report is that place matters and that all localities have unique qualities. This does mean that a one size fits all range of solutions cannot be prescribed from a national level. It also means that a new social contract between citizen and government needs to be developed at local, regional and national levels. The challenges facing different areas and therefore the solutions will be influenced by a range of factors including: history of migration and settlement, levels of poverty and wealth, de-industrialisation and the current population profile. We strongly believe in tailored and bespoke local activity to build integration and cohesion.

...

As a Commission we have been struck by the remarkable level of commitment that is focused on building stronger and better communities. From a spectrum of individual actions to those organised by the voluntary sector, faith organisations and Local Authorities the range of activity is impressive. The local focus of work moves forward in the context of a national government commitment to integration and cohesion. This is a welcome mosaic of activity and one that needs to be built upon, supported and enabled to make an even greater impact.

The most valuable contribution though comes from all of us as local citizens. Yes it is true that government – local and central – is essential to the mix of activity. It is also the case that the third sector is critical. However, it is through millions of small everyday actions that we can all either improve or harm our local communities.

...

As a Commission we have reviewed a huge amount of material and received helpful responses across a wide range of issues. We are very grateful for all those who have participated in our work. We have been overwhelmed by the quality and range of contributions. We have carefully reviewed all the material brought to our attention. However, given the breadth of material, we have had to prioritise those areas where we think recommendations would be most productive in moving our work forward. We have set out how we intend to monitor progress. We have also published on our website an analysis of responses to the consultation, and examples of case studies from across the country.

Darra Singh OBE, Chair of the Commission, in Commission on Integration and Cohesion, 2007, pp. 4, 5

As you read through this, we would hope that what particularly stood out for you was the mobilisation of the concept of *community* (mainly, but not solely, place based) as the site through which to generate and deliver the *policy* intention (social well-being, i.e. integration; and social stability, i.e. cohesion) and *evidence* (the Commission 'reviewed a huge amount of material': in fact, it worked through a massive consultation exercise, collected data on best practice case studies, commissioned MORI polls on local priorities and concerns, and committed itself to monitoring processes that rely on evidence to show policy effectiveness).

Our second example is drawn from the current social policy orientations of the World Bank. Again, the chapters in this book have detailed some of the ways in which international and global organisations have engaged with the concept of community as a means of delivering social welfare policy (Chapter 1 and particularly Chapter 2, for example). In this example, we consider briefly the World Bank's simultaneous emphasis on community, on policy and on evidence.

The extract that follows has been selected from the World Bank's 'Community Driven Development' (CDD) website. The extract is in three parts. First, it provides a brief *overview* of the way in which community features at the centre of the World Bank's CDD policy approach. Second, it provides brief details of a *specific CDD case study* – the Kalahi-CIDSS (Comprehensive and Integrated Delivery of Social Services) in the Philippines. Third, it provides the details of a forthcoming seminar providing *research findings* on the success or otherwise of the CDD strategy in the Philippines.

Extract 6.2

Community Driven Development (CDD)

Overview

Community Driven Development (CDD) approaches poor people and their institutions as assets and partners in the development process, and is broadly defined as giving control of decisions and resources to community groups and local governments. CDD programs operate on the principles of local empowerment, participatory governance,

Figure 6.7
Contrasting
communities: poor and
rich areas, Manila, the
Philippines;
'community driven
development': workers
on a local Kalahi-CIDSS
project in the
Philippines

demand-responsiveness, administrative autonomy, greater downward
accountability, and enhanced local capacity. Experience has shown that
given clear rules of the game, access to information, appropriate
capacity and financial support, poor men and women can effectively
organize in order to identify community priorities and address local
problems, by working in partnership with local governments and other
supportive institutions.

The East Asia and Pacific region has several CDD projects under implementation and others under preparation. The following [is a] representative [example] in ... the Philippines.

...

KALAHI-CIDSS Project (Philippines)

Implemented in 2003, the KALAHI-CIDSS* is a community-driven development project that aims to empower communities through their enhanced participation in community projects that reduce poverty.

Within 6 years, the project aims to cover 25 percent of the poorest municipalities in the poorest 42 (out of 79) provinces of the Philippines, equivalent to more than 4,000 villages in 182 municipalities. It strengthens community participation in local governance and develops local capacity to design, implement, and manage development activities. Community grants are used to support the building of low-cost, productive infrastructure such as roads, water systems, clinics, and schools.

*KALAHI = *Kapitbisig Laban sa Kahirapan (Linking Arms against Poverty)*
*CIDSS = *Comprehensive and Integrated Delivery of Social Services*

World Bank, 2008a

[The evaluation and monitoring of the projects is ongoing, as the seminar series mentioned in the next part of Extract 6.2 demonstrates.]

Social Development Department Seminar Series: Does CDD Work? Emerging Evidence from the KALAHI-CIDSS Project in the Philippines

Description:

Community-Driven Development (CDD) approaches are an important part of the World Bank's operations and are one of the preeminent means by which the World Bank supports the demand for good local governance. We evaluate the Philippines KALAHI-CIDSS operation as an example of a carefully designed, large-scale CDD project. In this seminar, we summarize research papers produced using a unique panel dataset of 2,400 households in 135 communities that was collected in 2003 and 2006. Through that analysis, we seek to understand who participates in project activities, how decisions are made by communities and, whether the operation improves local governance and enhances social capital.

Overall, we find that the preferences of community members and elected village leaders (barangay captain) seem to be equally represented in the community's project proposal. We also find that households that are more involved in communal activities are more likely to have their preferences represented in village proposals. Our evidence suggests that, within a municipality, resources flow to the poorest and more politically active villages. Finally, treatment by the project appears to markedly improve local governance and enhance social capital especially for those households who participate in project activities. These findings give insights into the social dynamics that CDD projects are working with.

Speaker:

Julien Labonne works as a consultant for the Community-Driven-Development and Local Governance Team of the SDV Department of the Bank.

World Bank, 2008b

We can see from this very different example the extent to which the concept of community has also been identified as the key vehicle for social welfare interventions and poverty reduction in the Philippines. Community is used as the basis for meeting a range of social needs, from basic amenities to health care and education. Community is also being mobilised as the means through which local people are active citizens and manage themselves in relation to social needs and social organisation. In the second part of the extract, we can see an example of policy-related research carried out by the World Bank, in this case focusing on the outcomes and effectiveness of the KALAHI-CIDSS project. Our concern here is not with the actual research findings, which are described in the third part, but rather to highlight the data collection that goes into evidencing policy effectiveness – that is, the importance for policymakers of having data to show 'what works' and what makes a 'good policy'.

We noted above that these are two different examples of the community–policy–evidence relationship, but we would also like to suggest that there are some underlying commonalities that both extracts share. In particular, what is striking are the expectations and demands that are put on the concept of community. Community is mobilised in these two examples as an instrument both for responding to social needs and for delivering civic participation, the management of difference, the resolution of conflict and social cohesion in local contexts. There is an expectation that these achievements will then effectively filter upwards and deliver social stability and order in national contexts. So, while the *divergences* in these two community-centred policy texts – cultural diversity and social cohesion in the UK and impoverished villages in the Philippines – are noteworthy, their *convergences* are also important. We can see community being selected by governments and global institutions as *the* conceptual and policy tool for the delivery of social well-being and social stability. We suggest, then, that community is ever more visible in diverse policy and spatial terrains. This ascendancy of community is reflected in the following comment from Graham Day:

> As recent calls for greater 'community cohesion' demonstrate, despite the many conceptual and empirical difficulties ... there is no sign that the term 'community' is going to go away either from the discourse of 'ordinary' people or from the rhetoric of those who seek to govern and manage them. On the contrary the capacity of community to mean so many different things, sometimes all at once makes it an invaluable political resource ... Discussions of problems of immigration, crime, terrorism, and anti-social behaviour rarely proceed far without mention of the part played by communities as either the cause or the cure.
>
> (Day, 2006, p. 233)

What Day captures particularly well here is the idea of community being identified as 'the cause or the cure' of social problems. This chimes with what has been a core concern of the chapters in this book – summarised by Allan Cochrane and Janet Newman in Section 2 of Chapter 2 as community representing 'both a "golden panacea" for the resolution of social ills, yet also the site of social problems'. Marilyn Taylor makes a similar argument when she notes that:

> While the renewed interest in community and the stable of ideas associated with it [e.g. social capital] is welcome, however, it is necessary to exercise some caution before hailing it as the answer to the world's woes. Pitting the David of community against the Goliath of international capital requires a huge leap of imagination or at least a dose of realism, especially when the Davids in question are the very people whom international capitalism has rejected.
>
> (Taylor, 2003, p. 217)

It is the multidimensionality of the concept of community, reflected in these comments, that lies at the heart of this book's broader efforts to shed the most effective and illustrative light on the nature of the entanglements between social welfare and crime control policies. In the next section of this chapter, it is to this that we return.

Figure 6.8
Examples of the ways in which community is explicitly visible and named as a social resource and provision in everyday local landscapes

4 Why community and more community?

All the chapters in this book – including this one – have argued that community has related but contradictory and multiple meanings. This multiplicity is in part the explanation for why community is such a charismatic and ubiquitous theoretical, everyday, policy and political concept. We have suggested throughout this book that it is community's ability to slip between offering welfare, care and stability and presenting exclusions, divisions and hostility that makes it of critical importance in the study of the collisions and convergences between social and crime control policy domains. Let us think back to Table 1.2 in Chapter 1, because this attempted to capture some of the key aspects of these multiple meanings and the ways in which they lead to and manifest connections with welfare and crime control worlds.

Activity 6.4

Reflect for a moment on Table 6.3, which has been adapted from Table 1.2 in Chapter 1. What is the dominant impression you have from looking at this overview of community and the social welfare–crime control relationship? Is it possible to identify and select those themes and definitions you would *most* associate with the concept of community? If it is possible, which would you choose and why? And if it is not possible, why is this?

Table 6.3 Four approaches to defining community

Approaches	Themes	Welfare	Crime	Thinkers
Community as a spatial concept	Face-to-face interaction in locality/place	Safe places Care Trust Social capital	'Problem' places Poor or 'wrong' forms of social capital	Tönnies Cantle Putnam
Community as non-spatial sites of identity and culture	Community formed through identity and imagined connections	Well-being Belonging Connectedness Social capital	Social exclusions Social disorders Poor or 'wrong' forms of social capital	Anderson Cohen
Community as boundaries and sites of conflict	Community as inclusion and exclusion	Social cohesion	Social divisions Social inequalities	Gupta and Ferguson Cantle
Communities as sites of citizenship and governance	Community as political investment and regulation	Social bonds Civic participation	Regulation Discipline Maintenance of social order	Putnam Etzioni Rose

Comment

It is likely that you found it a challenge to decide on a single, or even a dominant, meaning. As the chapters in this book have all argued, it is community's 'stretch' that lends it its appeal and usability across a variety of settings. And as Zigmunt Bauman (2001) comments, community continually eludes us at precisely the time that more and more of us all go in search of it and speak of it. For Bauman, the increasing precariousness and uncertainty of the contemporary social world pushes people to seek the apparently safe harbour of community, although its inherent elusiveness and fragility only serve to increase a sense of a lack of safety and security (see Chapters 1, 3 and 4; also **Cochrane and Talbot, 2008**).

What the table clearly presents – and what the material in each of the preceding chapters has examined – is community's ability both to describe and explain 'problem' places and 'problem' populations *and* 'good' places and 'good' populations. There is an inherent contradiction at the heart of the concept of community and, at the same time, there is an inherent coherency too – for example, social disorder is explained through the frame of community, but community is also identified as an instrument for maintaining social order; social disadvantage is explained through the frame of community and yet community is also identified as an instrument for addressing social disadvantage. It is this flexibility that means that community can so effectively illuminate the strange entanglements between social welfare and crime control. It is helpful to return to John Clarke's suggestion, in Chapter 3, that there are four core desires that underpin the concept of community – restoration, security, sociality and solidarity – because these can be mapped reasonably straightforwardly on to the social welfare–crime control relationship. For example, restoration and security link directly to crime control, and sociality and solidarity link directly to social welfare and well-being. This relationality is visible in all the chapters here. For example, Chapter 5 provided a discussion of the ways in which people enact community through forms of participation that may be convivial and social; or lobby to effect change in policy, politics and the local distribution of social resources and goods; or be disorderly and challenging to policy systems. Similarly, Chapters 2 and 4 examined the ways in which community has been at the centre of hybrid (i.e. social welfare *and* crime control) policy interventions. Chapters 2 and 4 discussed a number of these policy hybrids, which ranged from community safety to housing tenancy agreements and antisocial behaviour, as well as extending to other social order-related agendas, such as community cohesion, civic participation and community-driven development.

The contradictions and coherences concerning what community might mean have allowed it to become the focus of extended conceptual development. The most obvious example is the notion of social capital, which was discussed in Chapters 1, 2, 4 and 5. Increasingly, the ideas of social capital have featured alongside community and have seen it integrated into policy development on social welfare issues and crime control strategies. The same contradictions and coherences have meant that community makes an effective site through which groups and populations can be both managed and enabled to manage themselves. Chapters 1, 2, 3 and 4 have all discussed the notion of governance and in particular the arguments about the ways in which community increasingly takes up a predominant space in policy and political landscapes. Community lends itself perfectly to ideas of effective governance as people take on – and are encouraged to take on – individual responsibility for themselves, their families and the communities in which they live or with which they are identified in relation to social goods, reform and regulation. In this way, responsibility for well-being, social need, conduct and security across a range of sites becomes devolved away from large-scale institutions and organisations and relocated to smaller-scale, individual, family and community units. This is what concerns Bauman:

> Insecurity affects us all, immersed as we all are in a fluid and unpredictable world of deregulation, flexibility, competitiveness and endemic uncertainty, but each one of us suffers anxiety on our own, as a private problem, an outcome of personal failings and a challenge to our private savoir-faire and agility. We are called ... to seek biographical solutions to systemic contradictions: we look for individual salvation from shared troubles. That strategy is unlikely to bring the results we are after, since it leaves the roots of insecurity intact; moreover, it is precisely this falling back on individual wits and resources that injects the world with the insecurity we wish to escape.
>
> (Bauman, 2001, p. 144)

While such strategies may not necessarily always invoke or appeal to community, community, as we have seen, is often mobilised as a way of making sense of such insecurities and of offering responses to them. Again, we can recall John Clarke's scrutiny of the desire for community in Chapter 3, or the rural focus group conversations in Chapter 1, or the findings of the Power and Willmot study in relation to the importance of everyday acts of welfare and neighbourly care in Chapter 5. For Bauman, it is the political and policy devolving down of responsibility and culpability that is highly problematic.

We have seen across the chapters of this book the value and importance of small acts, but the local disconnecting of these from their wider social and economic contexts, means that small acts are unlikely, on their own, to be socially transformative and sufficient to deliver well-being, meet social needs, or provide social justice and security. However, as welfare states continue to be reconfigured (see Chapters 2 and 3; **Clarke, 2008**) with increasingly non-state and individualised approaches to social welfare and crime control policymaking, it is community that is being valorised as *the* way of 'replacing' state-based provision and enabling and responsibilising populations for providing their own social well-being and security. In this way, as we saw in our earlier focus on the Commission on Integration and Cohesion's report *Our Shared Future* and the World Bank's CDD policy, in Extracts 6.1 and 6.2, there are likely to be more, rather than fewer, demands on and recourse to community in current policy and political thinking in local, national, transnational and global contexts.

5   Community, welfare, crime and society

In this chapter we have returned to the questions that lie at the heart of this book. We have discussed how each of these questions has been responded to by the preceding chapters as they have engaged with the twists and turns of community, and we have suggested that community has an increasingly prominent place in everyday, academic, policy and political environments. We have argued that the multidimensionality of community and the absence of any consensus regarding its meanings, have, far from making it redundant, actually served to increase the diversity and intensity of its appeal in the contemporary world.

Any account of what community offers, in terms of explaining social relations and the policy interventions that surround and impact on social relations, has to take into consideration community's versatile ability to work as everyday (inclusionary and exclusionary) social practices, to shape policymaking and delivery, and to be a focus for social welfare and crime control institutions. We have seen community:

- drawn on as a resource for vulnerable, marginalised and dispossessed populations, and to organise and lobby for social justice-related entitlements

- sought as a way of establishing social order and security

- used to mobilise boundaries and 'us' and 'them' divisions

- used as an object of identity formation

- used as an object of hybrid welfare–crime policymaking

- enacted as social bonds and as practices of social care

- mobilised as a strategy for the management and containment of populations, and as a vehicle for devolving responsibility for well-being and welfare to particular populations.

The protean quality that community possesses is part of why it still demands commentary and analysis in the twenty-first century in the way it elicited commentary and analysis from sociologists such as Ferdinand Tönnies and Robert Park in the nineteenth and twentieth centuries (see Chapter 1). As Graham Day notes, 'it does not seem relevant to seek to legislate which of the meanings is more correct. Much of the interest lies rather in seeing how they are used to accomplish such different purposes' (Day, 2006, p. 245).

The question of what can be accomplished is, of course, a key driver in research on the concept of community and on communities themselves. This book has been concerned to engage with examples of the empirical investigations of the meanings of community and the effectiveness of community-based policymaking. It has argued that the connections between community, research evidence and policy development are well established. The chapters have illuminated the complexities, limitations, possibilities and successes of community and community-based social welfare and crime control policy delivery. However, the ambivalences that surround the concept of community and community-driven policymaking are unlikely, in the face of persistent levels of poverty, increasing social division and rising senses of insecurity, to deter community's ascendancy as the vehicle through which to define and identify social exclusion, disorder and disadvantage, and as the most likely instrument with which to respond to and deliver social inclusion, stability and well-being.

References

Bauman, Z. (2001) *Community: Seeking Safety in an Insecure World*, Cambridge, Polity Press.

Clarke, J. (2008) 'Looking for social justice: welfare states and beyond' in Newman, J. and Yeates, N. (eds) *Social Justice: Welfare, Crime and Society*, Maidenhead, Open University Press/Milton Keynes, The Open University.

Cochrane, A. and Talbot, D. (2008) 'Conclusion' in Cochrane, A. and Talbot, D. (eds) *Security: Welfare, Crime and Society*, Maidenhead, Open University Press/Milton Keynes, The Open University.

Commission on Integration and Cohesion (2007) *Final Report: Our Shared Future*, London, Commission on Integration and Cohesion.

Day, G. (2006) *Community and Everyday Life*, London, Routledge.

Taylor, M. (2003) *Public Policy in the Community*, London, Palgrave.

World Bank (2008a) *Community Driven Development (CDD)* [online], http://www.worldbank.org (Accessed 19 May 2008).

World Bank (2008b) *Social Development Department Seminar Series: Does CDD Work? Emerging Evidence from the KALAHI-CIDSS Project in the Philippines* [online], http://www.worldbank.org (Accessed 19 May 2008).

Acknowledgements

Grateful acknowledgement is made to the following sources:

Cover

Copyright © Sylvain Grandadam/Getty Images.

Chapter 1

Figures: Figure 1.1 top: Copyright © Bert Hardy/Hulton Archive/Getty Images; Figure 1.1 centre: Copyright © Sean Dempsey/PA Photos; Figure 1.1 bottom: Copyright © Nils Jorgensen/Rex Features; Figure 1.2 left: Copyright © Mel Evans/AP/PA Photos; Figure 1.2 right: Courtesy of Stockport Local Heritage Library; Figure 1.3: Copyright © Colin Palmer Photography/Alamy; Figure 1.5 left: Copyright © Jason Sheldon/PA Photos; Figure 1.5 right: Copyright © Anthony Neste/HBO/The Kobal Collection; Figure 1.6 left: Copyright © Rex Moreton/The Photolibrary Wales/Alamy; Figure 1.6 right: Copyright © Bubbles Photo Library.

Chapter 2

Text: Extracts 2.1, 2.2 and 2.3: Prior, D. (2007) *Continuities and Discontinuities in Governing Anti-Social Behaviour,* Institute of Applied Social Studies, University of Birmingham; Extract 2.4: Perrons, D. and Skyers, S. (2003) 'Empowerment through participation? Conceptual explorations and a case study', *International Journal of Urban and Regional Research,* Vol. 27.2, Blackwell Publishing Ltd.

Figures: Figure 2.2 left: Copyright © Rex Features; Figure 2.2 right: Copyright © Mike Abrahams/Alamy; Figure 2.3: Venning, H. (2005) 'Clare in the Community', *The Guardian* 1 June 2005. Copyright © Guardian News & Media Ltd 2005; Figure 2.4: Copyright © Sean Dempsey/PA Archive/PA Photos; Figure 2.5: By kind permission of the Cheshire Partnership Board for Adults with Learning Disabilities.

Chapter 3

Figures: Figure 3.1: Copyright © James Osmond Photography; Figure 3.2: Copyright © Rich Legg/iStockphoto; Figure 3.3: Copyright © Roger G Howard Photography; Figure 3.4: Reproduced by kind permission of Sefton MBC Leisure Services Department, Arts and Cultural Services, Atkinson Art Gallery; Figure 3.5: Copyright © Margaret Bourke-White/Time & Life Pictures/Getty Images; Figure 3.6: Copyright © J A Hampton/Hulton Archive/Getty Images; Figure 3.7: Copyright © Robin MacDougall/Photographer's Choice/Getty Images; Figure 3.8: Copyright © Eye Ubiquitous/Rex Features.

Chapter 4

Figures: Figure 4.1: Copyright © Steve Bell 2007, all rights reserved; Figure 4.2: Home Office (2007) *Cutting Crime: A New Partnership*. Crown copyright material is reproduced under Class Licence Number C01W0000065 with the permission of the Controller of HMSO and the Queen's Printer for Scotland; Figure 4.3 left: Copyright © Michael Stephens/PA Photos; Figure 4.3 right: Copyright © Howard Davies/Corbis; Figure 4.4 top: Copyright © Tim Wimborne/Reuters/Corbis; Figure 4.4 centre: Copyright © Greg Wood/Getty Images; Figure 4.4 bottom: Copyright © Christine Osborne/Corbis; Figure 4.5: Courtesy of Ronald Grant Archive.

Chapter 5

Figures: Figure 5.1 top: Copyright © Ray Tang/Rex Features; Figure 5.1 centre: Copyright © David Jones/PA Archive/PA Photos; Figure 5.1 bottom: Copyright © Martin Rickett/PA Wire/PA Photos; Figure 5.2: Copyright © Jenny Matthews/Panos Pictures; Figure 5.3: Copyright © Jean Adair/Govanhill Baths Community Trust Charity; Figure 5.4 top: Copyright © MAXPP/Philippe de Poulpiquet/epa/Corbis; Figure 5.4 centre and bottom: Copyright © Bettmann/Corbis; Figure 5.6: Copyright © picture reproduced courtesy of the *Telegraph & Argus*, Bradford (www.telegraphandargus.co.uk).

Chapter 6

Text: Extract 6.2: Copyright © The World Bank Group 2008.

Figures: Figures 6.1 and 6.8 bottom right: Copyright © Gerry Mooney; Figure 6.2: Copyright © Hulton-Deutsch Collection/Corbis; Figure 6.3 left: Welsh Assembly Government (2007) *Communities First Guidance 2007*, Welsh Assembly Government. Crown copyright material is reproduced under Class Licence Number C01W0000065 with the permission of the Controller of HMSO and the Queen's Printer for Scotland; Figure 6.3 right: Office of the Deputy Prime Minister (2003) *Sustainable Communities: Building for the Future*, Office of the Deputy Prime Minister. Crown copyright material is reproduced under Class Licence Number C01W0000065 with the permission of the Controller of HMSO and the Queen's Printer for Scotland; Figure 6.6: Copyright © Rex Features; Figure 6.7 top: Copyright © Friedrich Stark/Das Fotoarchiv/Still Pictures; Figure 6.7 bottom: Courtesy of Glenn Maboloc/Kalahi-CIDSS Project, Manila; Figure 6.8 top left: Copyright © Rona Scott; Figure 6.8 top right: Copyright © Jenny Meegan; Figure 6.8 bottom left: Copyright © Helen Kaye.

Index